Advance Praise for
PROJECTS THAT MATTER
Successful Planning & Evaluation for Religious Organizations

"The key word is *and*. Churches and religious organizations need to plan well to prepare for a future with limited resources. *And* they need to do good evaluation to discover what in their plan has and has not worked and to make the proper adjustments. This book will help them do just that. As the author states, 'Evaluation further deepens . . . how resources can be used more wisely.'

"This book offers a real gem that is so often missed by religious organizations: planning and evaluation are not two separate entities but one joint operation. Any successful plan must have built into it constant evaluation, and any worthwhile evaluation will lead to new directions and a change in plans.

"The five elements for planning a project *and* the six steps for effective evaluation contained in this book will ensure that any group enjoys a successful adventure. 'Good plans,' says the author, 'lay the basis for a strong evaluation design, *and* evaluations provide ways of improving a good plan.'"

Thomas P. Sweetser, SJ
Director of the Parish Evaluation Project
Author of The Parish As Covenant: A Call to Pastoral Partnership

"Kathleen Cahalan makes a provocative claim: religious groups that choose to plan and evaluate their programs carefully are practicing the spiritual virtues of stewardship, discernment, and prudence. She helps leaders cultivate these virtues in their own organization by providing step-by-step practical advice for designing projects, creating evaluation tools, and interpreting findings to various audiences. Her advice is rooted in a decade of professional work evaluating programs and teaching others how to engage in self-evaluation. If you're concerned with how to carry out your organization's mission effectively, you won't want to refuse Cahalan's invitation to explore how your organization's beliefs and traditions can shape a successful planning and evaluation style."

The Rev. Dr. Karen-Marie Yust
Christian Theological Seminary
Assistant Professor of Christian Education

Projects
That Matter

Successful Planning
& Evaluation for
Religious Organizations

KATHLEEN A. CAHALAN

An Alban Institute Book
ROWMAN & LITTLEFIELD
Lanham • Boulder • New York • Toronto • Plymouth, UK

First Rowman & Littlefield paperback edition 2014

Published by Rowman & Littlefield
4501 Forbes Blvd, Suite 200, Lanham, MD 20706
www.rowman.com

10 Thornbury Road, Plymouth PL6 7PP, United Kingdom

Library of Congress Catalog Number 2002116297

ISBN 13: 978-1-56699-276-3 (pbk: alk. paper)

∞™ The paper used in this publication meets the minimum requirements of American National Standard for Information Sciences—Permanence of Paper for Printed Library Materials, ANSI/NISO Z39.48-1992.

Printed in the United States of America

Contents

Foreword

Program planning. Evaluation. What could be more prosaic? These terms are not exactly inspirational. Their connotations are administrative (one is tempted to say, "merely" administrative), even bureaucratic.

But consider what is at stake—particularly in religious organizations! When people of faith start to imagine a new project or a program of some kind—whether it is a one-time event or a long-term effort made up of many activities—it is almost always in order to do something that will make a difference in people's lives. Jesus taught that two commandments summarized all the law and the prophets: "love the Lord your God with all your heart, and with all your soul, and with all your mind" and "love your neighbor as yourself" (Matt. 22:37-40). I suspect that behind virtually every endeavor undertaken by a religious organization there lies a hope that the new thing we do—or the ongoing thing we keep on doing—will, in one way or another, be an expression and embodiment of a fitting response to the call we hear to love God and our neighbors.

When religious organizations mount projects and programs, then, what is at stake is the efficacy of love and care and service. What is at stake is how human beings engage with and relate to one another. What is at stake is how minds are illuminated, hearts are moved, burdens are lifted, wounds are healed. And because so much is ultimately at stake, it matters a lot that the projects and programs be done really well.

That is where such seemingly prosaic matters as program planning and evaluation come in. There is no guarantee, but it is a pretty good bet that, when we launch and conduct the projects and programs that matter to us most, they will have a much better chance of doing what we hope they will if, right from the start, we think very carefully about what we are trying to accomplish and about how we think we can most effectively get that done. And it makes a lot of sense for us to be asking ourselves all the way along whether what we are doing is really making that difference, whether we really are doing it as well as it can be done, and whether we are in fact spending our selves and our resources on what really matters.

Kathleen Cahalan has written a splendid primer for all of us in religious organizations who need a little guidance as we plan our projects and programs, try to keep track of how they are going once they are under way, and look for ways to figure out whether they are meeting their marks. The help she provides is straightforward and clear.

"*A project* responds to a set of *conditions* by gathering *resources* that support *activities* that produce *results* that have an *impact* on people, and a *rationale* explains why this is so." Stop and read that sentence once or twice more. Once you "get it"—and the whole first part of the book will make it easy for you to do so—you will have in your mind an absolutely invaluable understanding of how to think and what to think about whenever you are involved in planning any kind of important event, project, or program.

Focus . . . design . . . collect information . . . discern and interpret . . . report . . . revise. Six steps. Once you have those in mind—and the second part of the book will make it easy for you to do so—a trustworthy way to learn from your own work, to assess its impact, and to build on what you have accomplished will open up for you.

I know all this from personal experience. As Dr. Cahalan says in her preface, the way of thinking about program planning and evaluation described in this book was borne of years of conversation at Lilly Endowment about how to do both of these things well. The ideas emerged through our work together and using them has made our work better. At Lilly Endowment, we plan grantmaking programs and evaluate them carefully. We also see thousands of "project designs" in the form of grant proposals and we fund hundreds of projects and programs. We try to support those that have a high chance of achieving important goals and of making a significant impact on the well-being of others. So, our work forces us to think carefully about program planning and evaluation every day. Dr. Cahalan stood back from the fray, organized much of our collective thinking into coherent form, and has now made the results accessible not only to all of you who read and use this book, but also to her friends at Lilly Endowment. We regard it as a gift and are very grateful.

This book contains a postscript. Do not miss it! Dr. Cahalan's "theological perspectives on planning and evaluation" are not just afterthoughts. They are foundational. Program planning and evaluation are not matters of mere technique. Nor are they simply tasks to be undertaken. Instead, as I said at the outset, they can be ways in which love of God and love of neighbor are embodied and expressed. When undergirded by serious religious reflection, discipline, and prayer, program planning and evaluation can be manifestations of our stewardship of the gifts that God has given us. Thus, for religious people and religious organizations, one challenge is to make our projects and programs as strong and effective as possible, because so much is at stake. But another, less obvious challenge is to carry them out in ways that reflect the kind of life together to which God calls us.

I hope you will find in this book helpful guidance in your efforts to address both of these challenges. I hope, too, that you will be encouraged by it to draw upon all the gifts of God's Spirit as you carry on in your profoundly important work.

Craig Dykstra
Vice President, Religion
Lilly Endowment Inc.
Indianapolis, Indiana

Preface

St. Paul's Church decided to expand its hospitality ministry several years ago. The new effort marked a significant shift from St. Paul's traditional practice of greeting people at the door and inviting newcomers for coffee and rolls. The mobility of young adults and families in and out of the parish called for creative ways of bringing newcomers into parish life; their frequent departures challenged the committee to think of ways to help people take leave of St. Paul's. The hospitality committee decided to pair a mentor with a newcomer who would help guide them into participating in parish life; a farewell committee was formed to determine how to help people make the transition from St. Paul's to a new home and parish.

After two years the committee began to ask itself what difference the new effort was making in newcomers' involvement and participation in the parish. Were people more likely to attend an event, join a committee, or serve in the liturgy if they had a mentor to help introduce them to the parish? Some committee members had concerns about the manner in which some mentors were guiding people: some were overly domineering, others hardly made an effort. What expectations did the committee have for mentors? What did newcomers need? Although committee members thought newcomers were being drawn into the community, some committee heads were complaining about being overwhelmed with too many volunteers, yet some newcomers showed very little interest in participating. The hospitality committee had some thoughts about the problems they saw, but these thoughts were based only on individual impressions, which were also beginning to conflict. Where could the committee get a reliable picture of the project? If the hospitality project needed improving, what should be changed?

St. Paul's experience of planning a new project and inquiring about its effectiveness could be multiplied many times over in religious organizations. Camp Longwood institutes a new marketing campaign to increase applications and attendance; Emmaus Seminary seeks to enhance the local community's awareness of the seminary's resources; First Church of Plymouth, a large downtown congregation, hosts a noontime lunch series on understanding religions. Religious organizations, like any organization, identify areas of concern and seek to respond effectively to those concerns, and they do so by creating new or modifying existing work. Likewise, people in religious organizations want to know that their work is effective and that it makes a real difference in the lives of the people they serve.

What makes religious organizations unique in comparison to other types of organizations is their religious mission and the way the mission defines their identity and motivates the work. A religious organization's mission reminds those within the organization as well as the greater public that its endeavors exist in relationship to a transcendent power. Religious communities name that power and are named by it—a Jewish hospital understands caring for the sick in relationship to Yahweh; a Christian school educates children in the name of Jesus Christ; a Buddhist relief organization cares for people in need according to the principles of Buddha. Each religious community's past as well as its future is defined in relationship to that transcendent power, and furthermore, the presence of Yahweh, or Jesus, or Buddha is a power that is ever present in the community's daily life. What this means for religious organizations is that even the most mundane and ordinary tasks, such as creating marketing plans, or hosting a noon-time series, or working with local community representatives, is infused with religious meaning and purpose. Religious organizations aim in two directions—toward the horizontal that encompasses the community in which they serve, and toward the vertical, the holy power under which they stand.

Another feature that makes religious organizations unique has to do with accountability. Because religious organizations are considered private in American society, they are largely accountable to themselves. Of course religious schools participate in accreditation procedures, religious hospitals and social-service agencies abide by government standards, and property owned by religious communities maintain public safety and fire codes. These external standards of accountability are necessary for religious organizations if they are to function at all in American society. But there is no external entity that holds a religious organization accountable for effectively carrying out its religious mission. The extent to which religious organizations carefully plan their work and assess their effectiveness is largely determined by their leaders. Religious leaders also determine whether planning and evaluation are understood as religious activities that support the organization's mission.

Welcoming and Taking Leave: St. Paul's Church

Expanding a Project with New Activities

St. Paul's is a large suburban parish of 3,500 families located near a fast-growing prosperous high-tech business development. Recently, new homes as well as office buildings have popped up on every side of the church, increasing the local population by about 200 percent in seven years. Because the parish has always been quite large, St. Paul's initiated a hospitality ministry many years ago. Initially it was quite simple: 10 members greeted worshipers at the doors of the church each Sunday morning. They wore nametags, greeted old members, and introduced themselves to new faces. The hospitality community sought to put a warm face on the community and strengthen the face-to-face interactions in what could otherwise be an anonymous encounter. Eventually, the hospitality committee began inviting newcomers, once a month, to coffee and rolls after worship.

But suburban sprawl and changing economic conditions were creating a new reality at St. Paul's: single young adults as well as families were moving in and out of the parish more rapidly than ever before. The church secretary was the first to notice: a person would join, and in two years, call to say they were leaving for another town; another family, who had been at St. Paul's for four years, called to say they needed to transfer their church records to a new parish; and, increasingly, mail was being returned "forwarding address unknown." Why so much turnover?

Church leaders also noticed that committees had difficulty getting new people to serve as volunteers. Attendance at parish events remained strong, but the same people seemed to be working all the time. Were new people coming to events, but not willing to work? Or were they not being invited to serve? Once church leaders began to see the relationship between membership turnover and participation, they decided to launch a project that would help newcomers become more active more quickly. The project took on the name "Hospitality for Discipleship," since the hospitality committee wanted to do more than welcome people; they wanted them to become active participants in parish life. The committee also began wondering what could be done for people when they left the parish. How could St. Paul's say good-bye and help people make a transition to a new community?

> The hospitality committee took up the challenge and designed two new efforts: a mentoring process that guides a new person or family in adjusting to the parish and local community, and a farewell team that would help people leave the parish. Mentors are trained to help newcomers identify ways to become involved in the parish. Mentors begin by getting to know the person or family, their interests, and previous church involvement. Mentors explain the parish's various ministries, and introduce the person or family to committees where their interests might match. Mentoring can last from 12 to 18 months, depending on the needs of the newcomer.
>
> The farewell committee was charting new territory. They began by placing an announcement in the Sunday bulletin asking parishioners to inform them if they were leaving the parish and when. The committee sponsored a quarterly farewell party to say good-bye to departing families. They also worked with the worship committee to create a farewell ritual that includes a blessing rite and sending commission. Finally, the committee developed a transition team to follow up with families after the move. Committee members keep in contact with the person or family for about six months. They make sure the parish has a forwarding address and they help people locate a parish in their new town, if necessary; the transition team members also make sure that church records are transferred in a timely manner.

This book introduces project planning and evaluation as mission-related practices for religious organizations. I think about planning and evaluation from a Christian theological framework, but the approaches to planning and evaluation suggested here can be used by any religious organization. In fact, I invite religious leaders to consider how their own faith tradition influences the way they plan and evaluate. In this book's conclusion, I make my own theological presuppositions explicit in relationship to a Christian understanding of stewardship, discernment, and prudence—three virtues that I think are essential for good project planning and evaluation.

Projects That Matter is a primer. It introduces project leaders and teams to a basic approach to project planning and evaluation. I intend the book for the nonexpert, those people who find themselves responsible for leading a project as well as accounting for its results. The focus here is on project rather than strategic planning. Strategic plans identify a variety of initiatives in relationship to an organization's mission, but that is only the first step. The initiatives, projects, or programs identified in strategic plans require detailed work plans and assessment strategies. Project leaders can use this approach to project planning and evaluation for several purposes: designing effective project plans, preparing case statements for donors or grant proposals for foundations, designing and implementing a project evaluation, and disseminating evaluation findings beyond the project.

Using *Projects That Matter:*

- implement aspects of a strategic plan
- initiate a new project
- prepare a grant proposal
- prepare a case statement for a development plan
- evaluate a project or elements of a strategic plan
- communicate project effectiveness to boards, outside constituents, and funders

There are three sections to the book. The first part is a basic overview to project planning. It guides project leaders in identifying five basic elements in a project design. Part 2 describes evaluation as a form of collaborative inquiry among organizational and project leaders that creates opportunities for learning and accountability. It offers six steps to implementing a project evaluation. Planning and evaluating are interrelated tasks: plans spell out the work to be done and the goals to be reached; evaluation provides an accurate picture of the work, how goals have been met, and information that can help leaders modify the plan as it moves forward. In this book's conclusion, I reflect on planning and evaluation from a Christian theological perspective—how I have come to understand this work as a form of stewardship in response to God's many gracious gifts.

I first learned about planning and evaluation by doing it. In 1993, I was invited by Jim Wind, who at that time was a program officer at Lilly Endowment, Inc., to evaluate a new youth project at Candler School of Theology—the Youth Theology Institute. I declined: I did not know much about youth or youth ministry, I was Catholic and did not know much about Protestant seminaries, and, most of all, I knew nothing about evaluation. "You bring gifts of discernment to the task. We can teach you the rest," was Jim's reply. The Endowment was seeking someone who could offer insight and wise counsel to both the YTI staff and the Endowment. They were asking an evaluator to help them think about a set of questions that sparked the seminary and foundation's interest in supporting a theological program for high-school youth: What significance did this approach to youth leadership development have for the church and the seminary? What can be learned by all those engaged and committed to this work—the project staff, the seminary, and the foundation—about inviting young people to think theologically for one month on a university-seminary campus? The fact that I knew little about evaluation did not stop me; my interest in answering the questions led me to accept the invitation.

Three years later, I was invited by Craig Dykstra, vice president of religion, to serve as the evaluation coordinator for the Endowment's religion division. My job was to identify people who could conduct evaluations of Endowment-sponsored projects; not an easy task as it turned out since most people gave me the answer I had given Jim Wind: "Thanks, but I don't know anything about evaluation." I began identifying and coaching evaluators in how to do evaluation; but gradually, I began to see a flaw in my approach. While an external evaluator could offer a much-needed third-party perspective on a project, projects themselves were often times not developing and executing their own project evaluations, at least not evaluations that were helpful and useful to them or to the Endowment. Often, project leaders were depending on the evaluator for information, rather than creating a body of insight and knowledge to contribute to an evaluator's review. Or, project directors had a great deal of knowledge and insight but were not recording and disseminating the information adequately. I turned my attention to helping grantees learn evaluation practices that would improve and strengthen their projects, as well as help others learn from their efforts, especially their boards and funders.

There are many people to thank for my education in project planning and evaluation. Craig Dykstra and D. Susan Wisely, former program director of evaluation, of Lilly Endowment, Inc., have been my teachers, mentors, and colleagues for the past 10 years. They helped me to see how evaluation can be an effective means of learning, and they applied that philosophy to their work as grant-makers. In 1999, we held a monthly evaluation seminar in which we read and talked about philosophical and theological ideas that informed our understanding of evaluation. These ideas, many of which shape this book, range from the works of Aristotle to H. Richard Niebuhr, and James Gustafson to Martha Nussbaum, none of whom are recognized experts in planning and evaluation, but who bring a wise perspective on both human nature and organizations. And, of course, these philosophers and theologians know something about the religious and moral life and how these factors shape human efforts and organizational structures for the good or ill, depending upon how intentional we are about guarding against corruption while maintaining fertile ground. Many of the ideas presented here are based on the experience and wisdom that Craig and Susan have brought to planning and evaluation, and this book is a result of our collaborative inquiry together.

I have also been fortunate to work with many Lilly Endowment grantees on evaluation, which has exposed me to a variety of religious organizations and their cultures of planning and assessment: congregations, theological schools, camps, and denominations. I wish to thank Don Richter, founding director of the Youth Theology Institute at Candler School of Theology; Carol Lytch, coordinator of the 1998 Theological Schools' Program for Strengthening Congregational Ministry, and the 67 theological schools participating in the program; Jim Waits and Melissa Wiginton of the Fund for Theological Education; Jacqui Burton and Corey Davis at the Institute for Church Administration and Management; and Mark Constantine, evaluator and consultant. I also want to express my gratitude to several Lilly Endowment colleagues who have helped me with this project: Elizabeth Lynn, Religion Division evaluation coordinator, and Susie Quern Pratt, associate evaluation coordinator; and Linda Engel, former evaluation associate. My editor, Beth Ann Gaede, at the Alban Institute also deserves special thanks, as does Alban's president, Jim Wind, who got me started on this path nearly 10 years ago. Dean Bill Cahoy, St. John's University School of Theology and Seminary, graciously allowed me the time to write this book. Without the help of these friends and colleagues over many years, I would not know today what I know about planning and evaluation.

PART ONE

Project Planning

Five Elements of a Project Design

A PROJECT responds to
CONDITIONS by gathering
RESOURCES that support
ACTIVITIES that produce
RESULTS that have an
IMPACT on people, and a
RATIONALE says why.

Everything I say in this chapter about designing a project can be summarized in one sentence: A project responds to a set of conditions by gathering resources that support activities that produce results that have an impact on people, and a rationale explains why this is so. Projects require plans because each of these elements—the condition, resources, activities, results, impact, and rationale—needs to be spelled out in relationship to each other. We can at times find ourselves involved in complex projects with only one or two elements clearly spelled out. Planners identify a set of activities with well-defined results but fail to explain how the activities and results are meant to impact the participants. Or planners may set forth grand plans for an event without considering the resources necessary to support the effort. And it is not uncommon for planners to articulate the impact they seek for participants but fail to explain why the activities will eventuate in the change sought.

As a teacher of pastoral ministry, I can neglect any one of these elements in the educational process. I can plan an engaging small-group experience but not define specifically what I want the outcome to be for the students; I can begin using technology in the classroom, but fail to recognize the amount of time it will take me to learn how to use the equipment, or how I think the learning experience will be enhanced by technology; I can define clear learning outcomes for my students but never explain how I think the assignments will create the kind of learning I hope will happen.

Is teaching a course a project? In a certain sense it is, even though it is a much smaller project than most organizations pursue. But the same questions must be answered regardless of a project's size. When I think about a course as a project, I must consider how it is an intentional effort meant to address a condition (the need for intellectual development of student ministers) through the use of resources (books, classrooms, my time and talent as well as the students', tuition) that support activities (discussing, lecturing, reading, and writing) that produce results (papers, discussions, number of graduate credits) that have an impact on the students and on me (increased knowledge, improved analytical skills, and deeper appreciation for collaborative learning). One of the greatest challenges I face is to offer a rationale for why I think students need to learn the material I put in front of them, through the learning strategies I employ with the results I ask them to produce—and why I think all of this will create the kind of knowledge and skills I think are necessary for pastoral ministry. When I take the time to answer these questions in the planning stages of a course, I know my teaching has a clearer purpose and that student learning will be enhanced.

A good project design, from a relatively simple plan to design a marketing strategy to a more complex plan to provide opportunities for interfaith dialogue at a downtown parish, contains five key elements: an assessment of the organization's capacities for the project and the project's relationship to its mission; the project's purpose and its goals in relationship to a condition; the activities and resources; the results the project hopes to accomplish and their impact on participants; and the rationale—a reasoned presentation showing why the project is necessary and why the organization believes it can successfully accomplish the tasks.

Camp Longwood has received steady applications from its denomination's congregations for the past 30 years, but in the past three years applications have declined. Additionally, the camp is receiving a significant number of applications from families outside the denomination. Several questions have emerged for the camp's director and board: What should be

Five Elements of a Project Design

1. Assess the organization's mission and capacities for the project.
2. Identify project purpose, including conditions and goals.
3. Explain resources and activities.
4. Determine results and impact on participants.
5. State the project's rationale.

done to encourage congregations within the denomination to send their children? Should the camp do more to encourage participation from those outside the denomination? If so, what does the changing makeup of the participants imply for the camp's religious formation and content? If both groups are to be recruited, what is the best strategy?

Camp Longwood's plan for a marketing strategy spells out each of the five elements in a project design. First, the camp's mission is to provide opportunities for growth in Christian service and leadership through outdoor activities for children from its denomination. Though they have never launched a marketing campaign, camp leaders believe they must find ways to communicate to pastors and congregations what the camp is about and why children should attend. Camp leaders face a particular condition that is both a problem (decline in applications from one group) and an opportunity (increased applications from another group). They determine that the goal of the marketing strategy is to introduce more of its denomination's congregations to Camp Longwood in order to increase applications from denominational families and communities. The marketing campaign consists of several activities: creating new promotional literature, establishing contacts with alumni, and designing a recruitment kit for congregations. The primary result will be a recruitment kit sent to 50 congregations; camp leaders hope its impact will be twofold—renewed interest and support of the camp from denominational members, and increased applications from its congregations. Finally, the rationale for the project is connected to the camp's mission: while the camp can continue to welcome and serve children from other churches, its primary mission has been to serve children from the sponsoring denomination. Despite other pressing demands on the camp's budget, its leaders argue that the future viability of the camp rests on a strategy targeted at denominational congregations.

Camp Longwood

A Small Project Aiming toward Significant Impact

Camp Longwood is a denominational camp that began in the late 1960s under the direction of two young pastors who wanted to create an outdoor learning experience for children. They served the camp for 30 years, and under their direction the camp flourished to serve 2,000 children, ranging from ages 7 to 14, in six different summer programs. When the founding camp directors retired about 10 years ago, the camp's board was faced with finding new leadership that could continue the success of the camp's programs; but they also needed someone who could respond to maintenance concerns requiring immediate attention.

During the first five years of the new camp director's tenure, Pat Conroy and the board secured financial resources to pay for the remodeling and updating of camp buildings. When contractors informed them the pool could not be repaired, camp leaders began plans to build a new swimming pool before the next summer. In the meantime, Pat realized a more serious problem than the broken pool. In reviewing applications for the next summer, he noticed that something was changing about the children who were applying to the camp. There did not seem to be as many children coming from the camp's primary feeder congregations. He looked back over 10 years of applications to determine how many children were applying, what congregations they were coming from, and who had recruited them. The findings were surprising. First, and most alarming, was a steady decrease of applications, from an average of 2,900 to 2,300. The decline had not been noticeable since some years had seen only a slight decline of about 3 to 8 percent; but looking at the numbers over a 10-year time span shed light on a lurking problem. Furthermore, the children applying to Camp Longwood from congregations outside the denomination was steadily increasing; to date, they numbered about 40 percent. When Pat presented the information to the board, he had many questions: What do these trends mean? Are we losing contact with the denomination and its congregations? Are we called to serve children solely from our denomination? If so, should we discourage applications and admittance to those outside? Or is our mission changing to become more ecumenical in focus?

4

➤ ELEMENT 1: ASSESS THE ORGANIZATION'S MISSION AND CAPACITIES

Organizations face the challenge of choosing between many strategies to pursue their mission. In fact, most organizations have so many good ideas on the table that they struggle to determine which ideas to pursue. When St. Paul Church began planning for an expanded hospitality program, the committee identified four possible formats, each favored by a different committee member. As with many committees, they came to a consensus, drawing out elements from each of the formats in order that everyone's ideas made it into the plan. When designing a project, it is certainly helpful for everyone's ideas to inform the design; however, good projects require more than committee consensus.

When an organization faces the task of choosing between several good options, the choice may become clearer by focusing on how each relates to the organization's mission and the organization's capacities for executing each option. The four options suggested by St. Paul's committee members fall equally within the church's mission, but they may differ considerably in terms of St. Paul's capacity to execute each successfully. Each option must be considered in relationship to the congregation's mission, the context of its ministry, the congregation's expertise in executing the project, and their ability to pay for it.

In the midst of deliberations over the various options, St. Paul's committee will need to answer a difficult question: Do we have the human, material, and financial resources to support any of the formats? In some cases, honest answers to this question may mean that good and creative ideas are left on the drafting table. Few organizations can run the risk of becoming overburdened with projects it does not have the expertise or resources to support. A good project design identifies how a proposed project fits within the organization's mission, how it fulfills a part of its strategic focus, and the resources the organization can commit to the project.

Assessing Organizational Mission and Capacity

- How does the project align with the organization's mission and strategy?
- Why does the organization believe it can launch this project successfully?
- What resources—human, material, and financial—exist to support the project?
- Are any additional resources anticipated?

➤ ELEMENT 2: IDENTIFY THE PURPOSE: CONDITIONS AND GOALS

The second element of a project design is the purpose. The purpose of a project consists of two elements: the condition that is being addressed and the response to the condition, which determines the project's goals and objectives.

Conditions

I use the term *condition* because it is broad enough to capture the variety of things a project can address: conditions may be a need or a problem but may also be an issue, question, or an opportunity. Camp Longwood faces the problem of declining applications from denomination-sponsored congregations, but an increase of applications from those outside the denomination could be viewed as an opportunity, depending on one's point of view of course. Religious organizations face a multitude of conditions: a congregation's attendance is dropping because of poor preaching; a college receives a gift to support religious artists; a denomination has insufficient numbers of younger candidates entering the ministry; or seminary educators lack a clear understanding of what Generation X youth think about ministry.

Conditions can be:
- a need
- a problem
- an issue
- a question
- an opportunity

Projects may be organized in response to a variety of conditions—increasing attendance, eliminating ignorance, or answering a perplexing question. Some conditions are practical in nature (attendance is dropping), while other conditions are less concrete and more speculative yet nonetheless real. (What do Generation X youth think about ministry?) Conditions require concrete responses because they place demands on a community—lower attendance threatens the vitality of the congregation; college administrators must identify artists who explore religious themes in their work and are interested in teaching college students; a seminary's program in recruitment and education is hampered by a lack of understanding younger students. Projects are the ways that organizations seek to initiate some change in a condition: they alleviate problems, respond to needs, or gain new knowledge into a situation. A project plan includes a description of the condition being addressed, who is affected by the condition, and the consequences should the condition fail to be addressed.

For example, First Plymouth is faced with an opportunity for which they lack sufficient experience and knowledge. As a large urban congregation located in the heart of downtown, they have been successful in drawing people to programs on the noontime lunch break—a series of concerts featuring musicians from various local communities; speakers on community issues; and ecumenical prayer services at holidays and times of crisis. They recognize that the city's population is increasingly multicultural and multireligious. Because of their location and past record of service, First Plymouth wants to host a series on interfaith dialogue, in the hopes that people from diverse backgrounds can come to greater appreciation of other traditions at the same time they see themselves as citizens supporting the city's common good. First Plymouth recognizes a need in the community, which they believe they can respond to and which is consistent with their mission.

But the congregation faces two challenges: they have never hosted interfaith dialogues, nor have they offered programs for their members about other religions. Where should they begin? Before the congregation launches into planning a noontime series on interfaith dialogue, several questions must be answered: What is interfaith dialogue? Who does it? What are some successful models in other congregations? How does a Christian congregation talk about other religions and talk to members of other religions? Will people from other traditions come to First Plymouth for dialogue? Do other communities share our understanding of the common good?

Opportunities, as well as problems, can raise many questions that left unanswered can result in faulty projects. Oftentimes, response to an issue requires research that helps project planners understand the condition, as well as the variety of responses possible, before determining the organization's specific response. The opportunity facing First Plymouth requires that project planners do some homework in order to understand the nature of interfaith dialogue in a congregational setting; with greater understanding, they can embark on planning a noontime series that fits their capacities as a congregation and the needs of city residents.

First Church of Plymouth

Initiating a New Project with Long-Term Goals

First Plymouth is a prominent church located in the heart of a major downtown city. For many years, it has been a tall-steeple church where prominent city and community leaders have attended. The pastor has long been engaged in ecumenical work in the city, especially in gathering religious leaders from various churches into dialogue and encouraging cooperative ministries between churches. The ecumenical council is quite active, and area ministers support one another in monthly prayer and discussion groups. Recently, they have been helping one another with preaching and taking the risk to switch pulpits on Sunday mornings in order that congregations might be exposed to a variety of good preaching and get to know area ministers. The ecumenical council has long believed that city residents should be able to identify a number of pastors who lead various faith communities.

During a yearlong strategic planning process, First Plymouth's minister and board of elders identified several strengths the congregation could build upon for the next five to ten years: a strong sense of congregational identity among the members; well-attended Sunday morning worship; an established Sunday morning adult education program; financial stability, and public recognition as an ecumenically open congregation. Church leaders recognize that First Plymouth, while not problem free, could continue on with business as usual and be content; or it could do something more. But what?

After a long discernment process, church leaders decided to challenge church members to take initiative, following the pastor's work in the ecumenical council, in initiating, leading, and expanding various ministries in the community with other churches. In particular, church leaders wanted to encourage more interfaith contact. Each area of the congregation's ministry—worship, education, pastoral care, and social concerns—was called upon to take up this vision.

The adult education committee had long faced a particular challenge in programming events: they have a good Sunday morning program, but as members moved from the city to the suburbs, the church has been less able to retain programs during the week, especially at night. After much discussion and planning, they decide to begin an education series at the noontime lunch hour expanding beyond the social types of gatherings the church has offered in the past. The series will focus on interfaith dialogue and introduce people to the city's various religious communities: the pastor or leader, the community's type of worship and ministry; its size, location, and history in Plymouth. The committee, as well as church leaders, believe that First Plymouth can become a center for dialogue and learning among people of all religious communities in Plymouth; by so doing, they hope people will gain a deep appreciation of religious pluralism that will lead to greater tolerance and enhance the city's common good.

Conditions are context specific. Planners aim for a complete and accurate description of the condition, which requires that they understand the historical as well as its present context. Camp Longwood faced a similar attendance situation 10 years ago, and camp leaders decided they could not spend the money on new promotional literature. In the case of First Plymouth, local religious leaders have been engaged in interfaith dialogue for several years, and a few have developed a curriculum for congregational use. In addition to the organization's context, the condition also has a larger context; other communities probably face similar conditions and are attempting to respond. History, as well, offers examples of successful and unsuccessful attempts to address issues and answer questions. Camp Longwood is not the first denominational camp to face the issue of who its constituents should be, and neither is First Plymouth the first congregation to face religious and cultural pluralism in its neighborhood. In most cases, some other community at present, or in another time or place, has faced a similar situation. They may provide leaders with wisdom about the complexity of the condition as well as effective responses to be considered.

Describing the Project's Condition

- What condition does the project aim to address?
- Who is affected and how?
- What are the consequences if the condition is not addressed?
- What solutions have been proposed or attempted by the organization and by others?
- How does the project build on earlier solutions?

Goals

Projects are, quite simply, a response to a condition or set of conditions. Projects are strategies and solutions that an organization believes can best address needs, bring awareness to important issues, or answer questions. Goals, then, are statements that define what the project will do in relationship to a condition. Goals spell out the kind of change a project aims to bring about in the condition: St. Paul's goal is to encourage newcomers to become involved more quickly in parish life; First Plymouth wants to strengthen the common good of the city by inviting people of various faiths into dialogue; Camp Longwood wants to receive more applications and support from denominational congregations.

Examples of Goals and Objectives

Camp Longwood

Goal 1:   *Increase applications from denominational congregations.*
Objective 1: Design recruitment kit for congregations.
Objective 2: Establish relationships with camp alumni from the past 10 years.
Objective 3: Target marketing efforts in 50 congregations.

St. Paul's Church

Goal 1:   *Increase participation of new members in parish activities and committees.*
Objective 1: Identify people to serve as mentors.
Objective 2: Create process whereby newcomers are identified and can join the mentoring program.
Objective 3: Match mentors and newcomers.
Goal 2:   *Assist people in making the transition from St. Paul's to another parish and community.*
Objective 1: Design a means of identifying members who are moving.
Objective 2: Work with the worship committee to create a blessing and sending rite.
Objective 3: Host a quarterly farewell party.
Objective 4: Develop a database system to track members' new addresses and the transfer of parish records.
Objective 5: Develop a means of helping people make adjustments to their new parish and community.

Describing Goals and Objectives

- What does the project hope to achieve (goals)?
- What has to take place for each goal to be realized (objectives)?

Remember that goals differ from objectives. Goals are distinct by virtue of their breadth; they are broad statements about the project's aims and purposes. Objectives are more concrete, tangible, specific, and at times measurable; they spell out the ways in which goals will be achieved.

➤ ELEMENT 3: EXPLAIN ACTIVITIES AND RESOURCES

Following a description of the condition to be addressed and the goals and objectives to be pursued, a project design includes a thorough description of the activities. It also includes a description of the resources that will support each activity.

Activities

Activities are work—the actions taken to fulfill each objective. Activities may include enhancing or creating new organizational structures to support the project (e.g., hiring personnel, arranging technical support); preparing materials (e.g., writing a curriculum, designing a Web site or promotional materials, preparing a book manuscript); or planning and hosting events, such as conferences, staff meetings, training sessions, or educational programs. Activities, of course, come in many sizes. Major activities, such as hosting a conference, can be broken down into many tasks—designing and mailing promotional literature, ordering meeting space and food, taking reservations, inviting speakers, producing resource materials, and so on. Along with identifying activities is the task of scheduling times and places for when activities are to occur and the cost of each activity. These elements, in relationship to one another, constitute a project workplan. Worksheet A provides an example of Camp Longwood's workplan, which details the project's first objective, four activities, and the people, time, and costs involved in each activity. (Blank copies of all worksheets are available in the appendix; planners and evaluators may wish to copy and use the worksheets for designing a project and evaluation.)

WORKSHEET A
Project Workplan: Activities, Schedule, and Resources

Objectives/Activities	Schedule	Personnel	Resources Time	Costs
Objective: Design recruitment kit				
Activity 1: Create new brochure	Fall 2003	Christi/Bob	4 months	Total: $30,000
Select historical pictures	September 2003	Christi	10 days	percent of salary
Collect stories about campers who became leaders in church and society				
Collect stories of prominent congregations who have sent campers	November 2003	Bob/designer	1 week	$2,000
Describe programs, emphasizing leadership development skills				

Objectives/Activities	Schedule	Personnel	Resources Time	Costs
Draft copy	December 2003	Bob/printer	2 weeks	$2,000
Hire designer for layout; design layout				
Contract with printer				
Activity 2: Design new logo and letterhead	Fall 2003	Bob/designer	1 week	$1,000
Activity 3: Create 10-minute video, emphasizing formation of Christian leaders	Spring 2004	Bob/video consultant	3 months	$15,000
Hire video consultant				
Select video footage of young people				
Write script				

Objectives/Activities	Schedule	Personnel	Resources Time	Costs
Activity 4: Redo web site	Spring 2004	Bob/web master	2 months	$10,000
Hire web master				
Update information about programs				
Include stories, pictures from camp's history and current programs				
Create a chat room for campers to stay in contact				

Resources

Resources support activities. A key resource in any project, of course, is money. A project budget is built on a realistic determination of each activity's costs, which includes people's time as well as materials. A project's resources, however, are more than finances. Resources also refer to the human assets an organization brings to a project: the gifts and talents of the people working on the effort. The organization may also have unique material resources that contribute to the project and key activities: a particular setting (downtown location), special facilities (100 acres of woods with three lakes), and unique assets (a history of pioneering adult education in the denomination). These kinds of resources are not neutral: like money, they are important factors in determining the quality and success of a project and its activities.

A detailed sketch of the activities, their respective tasks, and the resources needed to carry them out can give organization and project leaders a clearer sense of the organization's capacities to take on the project. It also sheds light on any gaps in the organization's resources: it may have the right people, but they do not have enough time; there may be enough time, but not enough money; the setting may be ideal, but the people do not have the right skills. In some cases, additional resources may be needed; project leaders will need to determine if outside resources are necessary to launch the project and begin to identify possible sources of support.

Describing Project Activities and Resources

- What are the main activities and how do they relate to the goals and objectives?
- What materials need to be produced, events planned, and organizational structures created or enhanced to support the activities?
- What is the schedule for each activity?
- How much will each activity cost?
- How much time will be spent on each activity?

➤ Element 4: Define Results and Impact

Results

After describing the activities and resources needed to accomplish the goals and objectives, a next issue to consider concerns the project's results and impact. There is an important distinction between results and their impact, which is sometimes referred to in the evaluation literature as "outputs" and "outcomes." Results (or outputs) are products produced by or events that take place from project activities; impact (or outcomes) describes what happens to people by virtue of their participation in project activities and results. For example, project results may include a new curriculum, the redesign of a Web site, a conference with 100 attendees, or a series of six noontime lunch gatherings. When projects state what they plan to do, or have done, in this way, the results tell us that something important happened or was produced, but it tells us little more. Stating results is not enough, because it does not offer an explanation of what kind of impact the results had on people. A new curriculum was prepared, but what did people learn from it? The camp had a 50 percent increase in applications, but what happened to the children who attended the camp? Offering a six-week adult education program in world religions is laudable, but what did participants learn?

Impact

Most projects set out to change what people think and do; that is, projects seek to impact people's attitudes and knowledge as well as encourage people to develop new skills and behaviors. Of course there is a complex relationship between learning new ideas and adopting new behaviors. St. Paul's hopes that newcomers will feel more welcome in the parish, and through a relationship with a mentor, become more quickly connected to the parish and its activities. Of course we realize that there are various levels of comprehension in learning something new: participants in First Plymouth's adult education classes on religious traditions may come to appreciate other faith communities but may not see immediately how they can work with other believers for the good of the city.

When considering the degrees of change a project hopes to achieve, time is a considerable factor. For instance, Camp Longwood's goal to increase applications from denominational congregations may take several years: congregations unfamiliar with the camp will need to learn about its programs, congregations who have sent children in the past will need to develop ways of identifying and supporting children to attend the camp; pastors who are camp alumni will have to become more intentional about recruiting young people for the camp. Camp leaders hope that a new understanding of its programs and new recruitment efforts by pastors and congregations will become established patterns of behavior. Likewise, First Plymouth will not achieve its goal of hosting interfaith dialogues overnight: it may require a year of research into other efforts, a year of teaching the congregation about other religions, a year of conversation with local religious leaders. It may, in fact, be several years before the main activity takes place and still more time for the goal to be reached; but the goal will be reached because of the kind of change that happens and accumulates over a course of time. Obviously if change is to be long lasting and permanent, significant degrees of change must take place over time. If a project fails, it may be because leaders have unrealistic notions of change: both the degree of change that needs to occur and the time it will take to affect such change.

A helpful way to think about change and time is through the concept of "impact." Impact is a way of talking about how the project activities affect people, particularly the people who face the problem, need, question, or opportunity. Project planners, in considering impact, must answer the question: How will participants benefit from and be affected or changed by participation in the project?

Remember that some impact is long term, such as enhancing the common good of a city through interfaith dialogue. First Plymouth will not be able to determine this kind of impact immediately; it may take many years and a variety of activities before it can be determined if anything substantive has changed about the people who attend the noontime series, the congregation who sponsors the events, and the city. If project goals are far reaching, and the final result cannot be known well into the future, planners will need to identify some of the significant factors that point in the direction of long-term change, as well as the activities that need to occur for such change to eventuate. Furthermore, long-term change in a condition may require more than the efforts of one organization; partnerships may need to be formed with organizations that have a similar commitment to change the condition.

Project planners can outline the relationship among immediate, intermediate, and long-term impact by constructing a sequence of causal steps: "if a, then b." The first step (a) identifies the initial activities, their results and impact on participants. The next step (b) requires planners to answer two questions: How does the initial impact build a base for the next kind of desired change that is necessary for longer-term and more ultimate kinds of change or benefits to accrue? And, what kinds of activities must occur in order that these further changes happen? A project plan describes the incremental steps of change that allows planners to claim how cumulative sets of activities building upon each other over the course of time produce qualitatively different kinds of change that eventually lead to the project goals. And a good project design offers strong reasons for believing that if "a" happens (certain activities), then "b" will occur (new knowledge, skills, and attitudes), and if "b" occurs certain objectives will be met that move the project forward to its goals.

Impact can be described in three timeframes: as initial, intermediate, or long-term impact. Whether impact is initial, intermediate, or long-term depends on its place in the sequence of events and upon what kind of impact is hoped for. The point is that a relationship among the sequence of events and anticipated effects is planned for—certain things must happen in order that certain results occur; certain results are necessary for the next set of activities to take place, and so on. If First Plymouth wants to strengthen interfaith understanding among city residents, parish leaders can begin with a few activities that establish initial impact, followed by intermediate activities that establish intermediate impact, and so on until eventually a long-term change in a condition is achieved. Worksheet B demonstrates how planners at First Plymouth mapped the initial project activities, their results and impact, and how they serve as the basis for the next round of activities.

Initial, Intermediate, and Long-Term Impact

- Initial impact refers to the immediate benefits or changes that accrue to participants, including initial changes in knowledge, attitudes, skills, or behaviors.
- Intermediate impact refers to substantial and significant changes in knowledge, attitudes, skills, and behavior that establish new patterns of thinking and behavior that are intentional, directed, and habitual.
- Long-term impact indicates a meaningful change in identity—a condition or status that persists over time.

Initial Impact

Initial impact is the most immediate kind of change project activities bring about. An activity may impact people in a variety of ways—parish members learn the purpose of interfaith dialogue; congregations are reminded of the importance of a denominational camp; some members of the congregation encourage young people to apply to the camp; newcomers learn about the parish's various ministries and volunteer opportunities. Initial impact plays a critical role in contributing to long-term change, but some organizations may realize that long-term change—as important as it is—is outside the reach of a single project or the organization's resources. For example, First Plymouth may realize that interfaith dialogue can eventually promote the city's common good in terms of greater cooperation between religious leaders and communities, but in the first few years of the project, that goal remains on the distant horizon. The best the congregation can aim for is to introduce people to a new idea and offer them an opportunity to consider what interfaith dialogue might mean in their congregation. Initial impact can make a real difference for people, and is an important kind of change; without this initial change in people's ideas at First Plymouth, any future work in interfaith dialogue may be in jeopardy. For some organizations, achieving the goal of initial impact is all they can do at the present time, and that is an accomplishment in itself.

If greater degrees of change are sought in a condition, however, more than initial impact is required. Let's consider an ambitious project at Emmaus Seminary to increase the seminary's public presence in the community. The seminary has identified a number of initiatives to support this goal. One activity is to host a fall festival and invite people from the neighborhood to meet members of the seminary community. Emmaus leaders hope the picnic will put "faces" on the seminary as well as its neighbors. They want the fall festival to have an impact on both groups: neighbors can ask questions about the seminary in a casual setting, and the seminary can learn about issues of concern facing their neighbors. The festival has a good chance of achieving this kind of initial impact, and it can provide a base that other activities with local neighbors can build upon. By itself, this initial impact cannot achieve Emmaus's long-term goal, but the relationships established at the festival provide an important basis for other things to now occur.

WORKSHEET B
Mapping Activities, Results, and Impact
Example: First Church of Plymouth's Project on Interfaith Dialogue

Initial Activities	Form committee to lead interfaith project →	Plan adult education classes on major religions →	Pastor approaches ecumenical council →
Initial Results	Four committee meetings Identification of five models of interfaith dialogue in congregations →	10 evening classes in Fall 2003 taught by university professor →	Pastor presents on project at December meeting →
Initial Impact	Members appreciate complexity of interfaith dialogue; understand a variety of formats they use; learn basic rules of dialogue	Participants learn basic facts about three major religions; learn to compare traditions; able to ask questions in non-threatening environment	Enthusiastic support by area pastors for the idea; pastors share concern that religious community needs greater understanding of each other

Intermediate Activities	Committee plans a format for a noontime series	Class participants visit faith communities and attend worship services	Ecumenical council proposes becoming interfaith council; subcommittee forms to explore options
Intermediate Results	Proposal presented at church council	10 people visit a synagogue; 15 people attend services at a mosque; 25 people attend services at Christian churches	Subcommittee presents report on interfaith councils
Intermediate Impact	Church leaders learn about the importance of dialogue; they are invited to critique the committee's proposal; both groups gain greater ownership of the project	Participants grow in appreciation of faith traditions in the city; learn behaviors appropriate to the customs of the people; get to know leaders from each community	Members learn what other cities have interfaith councils, how they function, the challenges and opportunities

Intermediate Activities	Committee sponsors a six-week noontime series, inviting a religious leader from six communities to introduce their tradition and its community in the city	Participants invited to serve as welcoming and set-up committee for noontime series	Religious leaders invited to serve as speakers for a noontime series
Intermediate Results	Six sessions held in Fall 2004; 50 people attend each session	15 people volunteer to serve	Six religious leaders speak
Intermediate Impact	Religious leaders are introduced to the community; participants learn about faith traditions and their activities in the city; First Church gains experience in welcoming people to its church	Volunteers exercise their leadership for First Church; they know and recognize some people from other communities; they use their knowledge of the other communities to create a program, decorate, and provide refreshments	Religious leaders learn to present their tradition and community to those outside of it; grow in appreciation of the need for more education

Long-Term Impact: Interfaith Dialogue Strengthens the Common Good of the City

The Public Image of Emmaus Seminary

Seeking Long-Term Change through Multiple Activities

Emmaus Seminary, established in the early part of the twentieth century, is a freestanding seminary located in an older urban neighborhood. It has a beautiful campus of about 10 acres, with lovely old buildings and a stunning chapel. It is a seminary that most people in the community, several decades ago, readily recognized as an important community asset. Faculty members were well known in the community, largely because the seminary, neighborhood, and much of the town belonged to the same denomination. Today, things are different: the homogenous religious and cultural makeup of the seminary and its surroundings are gone. Faculty come from several denominations, as do students, and the city and surrounding suburbs host a wide variety of churches and worshiping faith communities. What once could be assumed about the community's understanding of the seminary is no longer the case.

In the past, seminary administrators and faculty were key community leaders—city and community officials regularly called upon the seminary to lead community events. Recently, seminary leaders were shocked to realize they were not called upon during one of the city's major crises. A group of teens had been violently gunned down by members of a rival gang in a poor neighborhood not far from the school. Community leaders and police called upon the assistance of area leaders, and several pastors helped the community cope through the fear and sadness. For weeks and months after the events, community groups began to mobilize efforts to make the streets safer for youth, develop meaningful employment opportunities for young people, work to get handguns off the street, and find ways to strengthen family life. As the plans unfolded among area pastors and community leaders, seminary leaders realized they were left out. Did no one think to call upon the seminary's resources to help respond to these issues? Why was this the case?

Seminary administrators invited the board and faculty to reflect on the situation. Most agreed that many members of the seminary community were actively involved in responding to the crises, but that the seminary itself had not been called upon as an organization with important resources to share. Someone suggested the seminary launch a marketing campaign to improve visibility in the community. But the seminary wanted more than increased public image; they wanted relationships and they wanted to be called into service.

Seminary leaders decided to move slowly and cautiously, focusing first on building up relationships. They needed to get to know community members and leaders, introduce the seminary and its resources to people who might not know them, and let people know what the seminary could offer the broader community. The seminary initiated a three-part project. They decided to begin with something fun and enjoyable, where people could come to the seminary, enjoy the beauty, meet new people, and listen to music. They planned a fall festival and spring concert, strategically inviting members of the immediate neighborhood as well as community leaders. Written invitations were followed up with telephone calls.

A second part of the project involved listening sessions between community leaders and faculty. Rather than hosting the first meeting at the seminary, seminary faculty and students went to interview community leaders and attended meetings to listen to what people described as their most pressing concerns. A third part of the project involved identifying areas where faculty research could intersect with community issues.

Intermediate Impact

Intermediate activities and their impact aim to affect more substantial and significant changes in thinking and behavior that derives from steady incremental change, sometimes extending over many years, which can lead to fundamental changes in a condition. Intermediate activities and impact link together initial and long-term impact. If a project is addressing long-term systemic change, it is necessary to clarify the relationships between initial and intermediate impact and intermediate impact and long-term impact. For example, Emmaus Seminary believes its faculty can be a key resource to local community projects, but they are rarely recognized and utilized as resources by community leaders. Seminary leaders plan several activities they hope can build upon each other: meetings between faculty and local leaders in which local leaders describe the issues they face; identification of research topics by faculty that connect with local issues; support for faculty research; and, eventually, lectures and workshops by faculty to share their research.

Long-Term Impact

Long-term impact aims toward a change in identity: communities come to understand themselves in a different way because of changes in a fundamental condition. This kind of impact is farthest removed from changes a single activity can expect to create, but it often is the kind of impact that leaders care most about and want to effect if real life conditions are to be addressed in any way more than on a temporary or piece-meal basis. In the case of Emmaus Seminary, a sign of long-term impact and change would be evident when (1) community groups think to call the seminary for assistance when addressing a problem, and (2) the seminary has the local community in mind as one of its primary constituencies when planning programs and supporting faculty research. It will take several years to change the notions the community has about the seminary and the seminary has about the community—attitudes have to change; strong working relationships will have to develop, and successful projects will need to be sustained.

Determining Impact

- What results are anticipated from each of the project activities?
- What impact does the project aim for and who will be affected?
- How will the project impact the sponsoring organization, its leaders, and participants?
- What kinds of activities must occur in order that further changes happen?
- How do cumulative sets of activities building upon each other over the course of time produce different kinds of change that eventually lead to the desired impact, whether it is intermediate or long-term?

Mapping the relationships among project activities, resources, and impact helps to show how the project's activities comprise a coordinated effort that can reasonably expect to culminate in many of the intended results. But a note of caution is necessary. A cause-effect model such as "if a, then b" is heuristically helpful for understanding the relationship between project activities and impact, but its predictive value is limited. Project plans should describe the kind of change project activities are designed to bring about, but there are many variables that influence change that cannot be anticipated and planned for. Project leaders must also be alert to the fact that projects can influence people in unintended ways, and factors outside the project can influence the results. As will be discussed later, evaluation is one way for leaders to identify a range of factors influencing the project's results.

➤ ELEMENT 5: STATE THE RATIONALE

The last step—stating the project's rationale—is not a separate step so much as an amplification of the argument that shapes the previous four steps. Projects require a rationale—a set of reasons that support the project's basic claims: why the organization supports a project and why it believes it has the capacity to carry it out; why certain goals have been selected to address a condition; why activities have been chosen and why the organization has the resources to support activities; and, finally, on what grounds the project claims "if a, then b."

A rationale often remains implicit until someone asks, "Why are you doing this project?" When an organization seeks financial assistance from donors or foundations, they are asked to make the project's rationale explicit. In addition to case statements, grant proposals, and accrediting reports, project leaders may want to write out a rationale along with the project's design in order to gain greater clarity and agreement about the project and why the organization supports it.

A rationale makes explicit the assumptions and arguments that stand behind a project. A project advances certain claims about the condition, its response, and the supporting organization. Claims are made reliable by offering evidence that supports the description of the condition, as well as the consequences for the community if the condition is not addressed. The evidence to describe the condition may include personal testimonies, findings from research studies, and statistical analyses. The evidence substantiates the claims that the condition is real and the consequences serious enough to merit intervention.

A project also makes claims about the organization's response to a condition. The rationale defines why certain activities have been selected by a project. Planners typically consider a number of options for addressing a condition, but any plan has limits in terms of what it can do: the rationale

26

spells out why a particular set of activities has been selected from a range of possible solutions. The rationale further explains why the organization believes these activities have the best chance of achieving the results and impact. Project leaders can explain the connection between activities and their results and impact. Building on the example from worksheet B, First Plymouth describes the project rationale in the following way; remember, the long-term impact they hope to achieve is enhancing interfaith dialogue and understanding among city residents in order to strengthen the common good.

- If a committee of talented congregational members is formed to undertake research on interfaith dialogue in congregational settings, the committee will be able to identify various models of dialogue.
- As the committee compares these models, they can consider what elements might best fit First Plymouth and the city.
- As the committee designs a noontime series, they can ask for input from religious leaders from neighboring churches and faith communities.
- Along with developing a noontime series, the committee recognizes that their own congregation requires more knowledge about other faiths; so, if adult education classes are offered for the congregation on various religious traditions, participants will gain knowledge of other tradition's beliefs and practices.
- If these participants attend worship services at synagogues, mosques, and churches, they will meet people and gain firsthand experience of communities in the city.
- If these participants have greater knowledge and exposure to various religions, they will be better able to participate in supporting and executing the noontime series with greater sensitivity and knowledge.
- If the noontime lunch series engages people in interfaith dialogue, participants will learn about religious communities in the city, and become aware of the distinctive aspects of each community as well as what they hold in common as citizens.
- If city residents can learn about religion in Plymouth, they will be more likely to find ways of working together for the good of the city.

A project also makes claims about the capacities of the organization— why it believes it has the resources to respond to this condition and carry out these activities. To strengthen the organization's case, the organization may need to provide evidence, particularly to funders, donors, and accrediting agencies, that the organization has the people, time, materials, and financial capacity to do the work. Evidence may include a proven track record in similar kinds of work.

A rationale requires discernment into the present situation—an accurate reading of the condition—and a realistic assessment of what a project can do to address the situation. Good project designs articulate the organization's judgments about what to do, in what ways, and why. Few religious organizations have sufficient resources to tackle all the problems and answer all the questions that face them. Leaders owe it to the organization, and its constituents, to debate, articulate, and refine a project's rationale in order to demonstrate that a project is worth embarking upon at this point in the organization's history.

Identifying the Project's Rationale

- Why have the project activities been selected from among various other possible options?
- On what basis is it believed that these activities have the best chance of achieving the project outcomes and goals?
- Why will the stated results eventuate from the activities and resources?
- What evidence can be given to support the project's claims?
- What are the limits of the effort?
- Given limited resources, in what ways is the proposed work critical to the organization in light of other competing demands on organizational resources?

At the beginning of this chapter, I said that the main elements of a project plan could be summarized in one sentence: A project responds to a set of conditions by gathering resources that support activities that produce results that have an impact on people, and a rationale explains why this is so. If project leaders keep these elements in mind in planning and executing a project, they can be confident that a project will have clearer focus and a better chance of achieving its goals.

Key Points of Project Planning

- A project is an organization's response to a condition or set of conditions.
- Conditions can be a need, a problem, an issue, a question, or an opportunity.
- Resources support the activities that respond to the condition; they consist of time, money, and people.
- Activities are the actions taken to fulfill the project's objectives that produce a set of results.
- Results are the products that eventuate from activities and have an impact on people.
- Impact is the way people are changed from activities and results, which includes new attitudes, knowledge, or skills.
- A rationale explains why a project claims what it does about conditions, resources, activities, results, and impact, and why an organization claims the project.

PART TWO

Evaluation as Collaborative Inquiry

Six Steps to Effective Evaluation

Before planning the third season of the hospitality project, St. Paul's minister of outreach suggests at a committee meeting that an evaluation might help the group to make improvements for the upcoming year. Committee members nod in agreement. One enthusiastic member suggests, "Let's design an evaluation form participants can fill out at the end of each session." Another member offers a dose of realism: "Great idea, but we don't have the time or the expertise to make up a survey. Let's just hire an expert in evaluation." A third member opposes the very idea: "What a waste of time, we already know how it's going and what we need to do for next year." And a fourth member dares to voice an underlying concern of many: "Are we sure we want to ask people what they think? What if the wrong people speak up and they distort what is really happening? Won't that possibly harm the project?"

The committee members' responses reveal some common attitudes about evaluation: it consists of immediate feedback after an event; it is extra work added on to an already full agenda; it requires experts; and it's challenging or possibly dangerous. Each of these attitudes reveals an element of truth about evaluation; however, they are not a complete or adequate picture of what evaluation is and what it can do for a project. Evaluation is much more. I think of evaluation as a kind of collaborative inquiry that builds on three important dimensions of strong organizations—learning, leadership, and accountability.

Standard textbooks in evaluation define the word *evaluation* in one of three ways: to assess the worth or merit of a particular object (Is this project worthwhile?); to assess objectives and outcomes (Did the project do what it promised?); or to gather information in order to make decisions (Based on what we know about the project, what aspects should be improved, added, or discontinued?). Each of these definitions highlights an important aspect of evaluation, but there is another dimension that I think supports all three. It might be best described as a meta-purpose—why an organization engages in assessment and decision making. The primary motivation to engage in project evaluation is a desire to learn.

But what does a project and organization seek to learn from evaluation? Quite simply, a comprehensive approach to evaluation allows us to learn something about each aspect of a project's design and, in so doing, contributes to the refinement of the project's rationale. Evaluation builds up a body of knowledge that can help project leaders refine activities, select appropriate resources, identify results, describe impact, and hopefully understand more fully the condition being addressed. For example, project evaluations can teach us something about the relationship among activities, resources, and impact: what resources are necessary to successfully undertake an activity, and what is the activity's real impact on participants. In short, what we learn from evaluation can become the evidence that further substantiates the project's claims about the condition it is addressing, as well as what the project is doing to address it.

St. Paul's Church claims that hospitality is necessary in a large parish where people have a hard time meeting others face to face. The hospitality committee believes that newcomers need immediate assistance in finding their way into parish life. Furthermore, the church believes that mentoring relationships are the most effective means of connecting people to parish activities. As the committee looks to evaluate their efforts, they can begin with the question: What is it we most want to learn about our project? Committee members might be wondering about a number of issues: What areas of parish life are newcomers attracted to and what are they most likely to become involved in? How do existing ministries welcome newcomers and draw on their knowledge and experience? Do any newcomers take initiative to start new groups and ministries? Questions such as these illustrate what project planners might desire to learn, and evaluation is one of the most effective means by which people can learn about their work together.

Many of us are accustomed to filling out an evaluation form at the end of a meeting, event, or conference. It provides the host with immediate feedback on what people liked and disliked. Often times this is valuable information and an effective means for gathering participants' immediate feedback, but in most cases it does not constitute the full range and scope of evaluation.

When evaluation is a means to learning, it is both a formative and summative practice. Evaluation that occurs over the course of a project is generally referred to as formative evaluation; when evaluation occurs at the conclusion, it is called summative evaluation. Both types of evaluation provide helpful ways of seeing what happens in a project. Formative evaluation, for instance, gives project leaders an accurate picture of what is taking place as the project activities unfold, and may assist them in making changes over the course of the project that will insure goals are met. Summative evaluation looks back on a project and seeks to learn how and in what ways project goals were met and what kind of impact the project has had on its participants. Summative evaluation is often used for purposes of accountability or accreditation. It also provides information to strategic planners that can aid in decision making about future efforts. Evaluation, then, can have a broad scope beyond the evaluation forms we are asked to fill out at the end of a conference.

If evaluation is going to do what I claim it can, it matters who in an organization is responsible for it: who leads it, who cares about it, and who uses it. Evaluation is the responsibility of organization and project leaders who help staff members, board members, and constituents understand that evaluation is important and useful. Leaders set a tone for evaluation; their attitude toward learning influences how others will receive and use evaluation information. It is no surprise that evaluation is often resisted; it can be threatening! A project, in fact, may not be living up to its claims, or securing the results it aimed for. Some people fear that evaluations will turn up negative findings that will lead to punitive measures against the project or organization. Others, on the basis of previous experience, may view evaluation as a waste of time and of little use. And some may see evaluation primarily as additional work on top of an already full set of tasks.

Evaluation may feel for some like negative judgment or being graded on their performance. A project leader may feel they have to prove something to others in order to get high marks. It can be uncomfortable to have a project judged, particularly in regards to work we care deeply about. We might feel that evaluators are looking over our shoulder and pointing out problems and failures. Because of our close involvement and commitment to the work, we may hear criticism or suggestions as negative indictments rather than as constructive proposals. And we may fail to separate what the project is and does from our personal investment and contributions to it.

Leaders can reframe evaluation to help overcome these resistances. For instance, when evaluation is truly understood as learning, the project's weaknesses, mishaps, and failed attempts are not threats, but opportunities. Leaders can invite people to step back and reflect on the project's goals, and identify the obstacles that are blocking success. If leaders allow people to see the project design as flexible and adaptable, evaluation opens up alternative strategies and activities. In fact, if plans do not change over the course of a multiyear project, it may be a signal that learning is not taking place. Because every element of a successful project cannot be identified at the outset, evaluation is indispensable for answering the questions: What have we learned from the project thus far? What's missing from what we are doing? and What needs to change?

In addition to a spirit of learning and openness, leaders can insure that evaluation is worth the time it takes. Evaluation is an activity that requires resources such as time, money, and material goods, so people must be able to see that the use of additional resources has merit for the project and organization. In essence, evaluation can create a spirit of collaborative inquiry among the project's stakeholders. A key aspect of evaluation is determining who these stakeholders are, what they want to learn, and how the project can engage them in conversation. Again, in a well-designed project, stakeholders are people invested in the project's rationale: they are committed to helping the organization successfully execute activities, secure needed resources, and achieve the results and impact necessary for changing a condition. Evaluation is a way to provide comprehensive information to the project's stakeholders so that they see more clearly, understand more fully, and learn what is necessary to do the work effectively.

Evaluation is a means of being accountable to the organization's mission and the project's purposes. Obviously, few organizations have the luxury to be wasting time and resources on unnecessary or ineffective projects. Evaluation helps to build the case for a project and strengthen an organization's commitment to sustaining it over the long term.

Project evaluation, then, has the potential to make good projects better. It increases understanding about the conditions the project seeks to address, and strengthens the claims about the activities and resources necessary for effective response. In addition, project evaluation helps us to see the project's impact on constituents and the organization. In essence, evaluation helps to refine the rationale that provides a project with meaning, purpose, and direction.

The next section presents six steps of project evaluation. The steps are sequential, progressing from one set of activities to the next. In most cases, steps 1 and 6 are the responsibility of project leaders who help to define the purpose and audience for the evaluation (step 1) and disseminate the findings to stakeholders and other audiences (step 6). Steps 2, 3, 4, and 5 are the responsibility of the person or team designated to carry out the evaluation, and they include identifying, gathering, interpreting, and sharing information from evaluation findings. The six steps constitute a cycle of work that requires time for planning, patience in executing, and a commitment to learning.

Focus

Design

Collect
Data

Analyze &
Interpret

Report

Revise
Rationale

Focus ◀
Design
Collect Data
Analyze & Interpret
Report
Revise Rationale

Step 1
Focus the Evaluation

- Determine the subject and purpose of the evaluation.
- Describe the audiences the evaluation seeks to inform.
- Identify key evaluation questions.
- Select a person to lead the evaluation.

The first step in project evaluation is for project leaders to define four basic issues: the subject, purpose, and audience of the evaluation, and the person assigned to lead the evaluation. Focusing the evaluation is a process that requires time to refine what the evaluation is doing and for whom. Because the answers are not always clear at the outset, particularly for large projects that include numerous activities taking place over several years, focusing requires that project leaders clarify the scope and intent of the evaluation. A clear focus at the first step will help insure a good and useful evaluation at the project's conclusion.

SUBJECT

The subject of the evaluation is the matter to be evaluated. At first, it might seem obvious to say the subject of the evaluation is "the project," however, projects have many components and all may not need to be evaluated, at least not at the same intensity or in the same timeframe. The evaluation may focus on particular activities, resources, results, or impact. For example, St. Paul's hospitality committee chooses to evaluate the mentoring relationships because they want to determine how effective mentors are in guiding newcomers into parish activities. First Plymouth will evaluate the courses on religion and visits to various houses of worship to determine what congregants have learned that can contribute to the congregation's noontime series.

Because some projects are large and complex, it can be overwhelming to imagine that every aspect of the project requires evaluation. Some aspects of the project may require evaluation at certain times but not others. Likewise, some activities or resources may be evaluated through other kinds of organizational assessment, and will not need to be repeated in a project evaluation. Emmaus Seminary, for instance, reviews faculty research through regular channels of faculty review; additional assessment is not necessary for its project.

Describing the Subject Matter of the Evaluation

- What is the subject of the evaluation?
- What activities make up the subject?
- Why is it important to evaluate this aspect of the project?

PURPOSE

There are many ways in which evaluation facilitates learning and collaboration among the project's stakeholders. The purpose of the evaluation is a statement about its overall intent and function in relationship to the evaluation's subject and audiences. An evaluation can do one or more of the following: describe and assess the quality and effectiveness of project activities and results; determine what objectives have been met in relationship to project goals; suggest improvements in activities and resources; understand the project's impact on constituents; and analyze the project's overall strategy.

Purposes of Evaluation

- Describe the quality and effectiveness of activities, resources, and results.
- Identify how well objectives are being or have been achieved.
- Improve activities and resources.
- Understand impact on participants.
- Analyze strategy.

The purpose of St. Paul's evaluation is to understand the quality and effectiveness of the hospitality program. The committee members want to determine what is most effective in mentoring relationships in order to improve what mentors are doing. Emmaus Seminary is focusing on the quality of the fall festival and spring concerts in the hopes of learning how many people from the neighborhood attended the events and why they came. An evaluation may shed light on each of the purposes listed above; however, the evaluation's main purpose should be focused on one or two, and should be stated in clear and specific terms.

Evaluation Purpose and Audience

- What are the primary purposes of the evaluation?
- Who are the main audiences for the evaluation?
- What are they most interested in learning from an evaluation?
- Why are these questions and concerns important to the audience?

Camp Longwood plans to evaluate its promotional strategies in order to see if their main objective of increasing applications is reached. The audience for the evaluation includes the camp director and staff, the camp's board of directors, and denominational officials responsible for camp ministries. The camp director and staff, who are responsible for developing the recruitment kit, want to learn how effective the materials are in communicating information about the camp; the board of directors wants to know to what extent denominational congregations will support the camp; denominational officials seek information that helps them understand the viability of the camp and the network of denominational relationships that support camp ministries.

AUDIENCE

The audience for an evaluation follows from the first two questions about the evaluation's subject and purpose: what is being evaluated, why, and for whom? The audience for an evaluation usually involves the project's stakeholders; that is, any person or group who has a stake in the project, who wants to draw insights and conclusions, make judgments, or take action appropriate to their role in the project. Audiences should not be considered passive recipients of evaluation, but rather, active contributors to both the evaluation design and its activities. Audiences play an important role in the evaluation design because their questions form the basis of the evaluation. In addition to forming questions, audiences are often involved in contributing information about the project. Furthermore, part of the evaluation design is determining how and when each audience will have an opportunity to discuss evaluation findings. Evaluation findings are more likely to be used and accepted when audiences are active contributors to the overall evaluation—design, data collection, and learners.

Each audience may have specific concerns about the project. For example, a project director and staff often seek information that helps them improve the project; board members look for information that demonstrates that a project is worth being supported and sustained in the future; funders seek knowledge about the ways in which program goals were achieved and the impact the project has had on participants and the organization.

In most cases, evaluations aim toward a few audiences—two or three at the most. Why such a limited number, if evaluation is meant to help people learn? Evaluations are less successful and meaningful if they try to answer too many questions for too many audiences. In other words, evaluations are more helpful and useful if they have a clear but limited focus. This does not mean that evaluation findings cannot be used beyond the primary audience. In fact, it is helpful to define primary and secondary audiences: primary audiences are those people who need immediate and concrete information from the evaluation; secondary audiences are interested publics that can learn something from what the project is doing and can receive information through various forms of public dissemination. A further way to distinguish the two kinds of audiences is to say primary audiences learn directly from the evaluation; secondary audiences learn from project leaders who disseminate information based on evaluation findings.

Audiences may include:

- participants
- project leaders and staff members
- organization's governing board
- related organizations and the community
- foundations and donors

IDENTIFY KEY QUESTIONS AND POTENTIAL SOURCES OF INFORMATION

An evaluation is designed to answer key questions that are directly related to the evaluation's purposes and audiences. The following list of questions, stated in broad terms, is based on the purposes described earlier; the questions may be refined and expanded to fit the specific concerns of a project evaluation.

The list of questions contains two basic types of questions: descriptive and evaluative. Descriptive questions seek to provide an accurate picture of project objectives, activities, resources, results, impact, and strategies: What are the main activities of the project? What resources support these activities? What objectives have been achieved? Evaluative questions focus on assessing the strengths, weaknesses, and merits of each aspect of the project: What are the strengths and weaknesses of each activity? What barriers exist to achieving objectives and goals? Evaluation questions also aim to understand the kind of influence a project has achieved, and the factors that most likely contribute to that influence; some factors contribute to projects in positive ways, and some in negative ways (e.g., What factors have led to the intended as well as the unintended impact?). The factors may be internal or external to the project, and an evaluation can help project leaders locate these factors, and understand how they are affecting project outcomes.

Impact evaluations look at the project's influence on people over time. They are particularly challenging because evaluators must track participants to determine how the project has made a difference in their lives, sometimes beyond the immediate and direct influence of a project. An impact evaluation of St. Paul's project would require that evaluators track the progress of participants through the mentoring phase, and who go on to become actively involved in the parish and serve on a ministry team. Worksheet C shows the relationship between the key elements of St. Paul's evaluation of the hospitality project: its subject, audiences, purposes, and key questions.

People often assume that evaluation begins at step 3—collecting data through interviews or surveys. But data collection cannot begin until the evaluation questions are stated. Define the evaluation questions first, and then proceed to collect information that will answer the questions. The key questions will help to determine some of the methods to use and the

Examples of Key Questions

Quality and Effectiveness of Activities, Resources, and Results

- What are the main activities of the project?
- What are the strengths and weaknesses of each activity?
- What resources support the activities?
- To what extent are the resources sufficient or deficient?
- What has resulted from each activity?

Achievement of Objectives and Goals

- What objectives have been achieved?
- What contributes to the achievement of project objectives and goals?
- What objectives have not been achieved?
- What barriers exist to achieving objectives and goals?

Improvements

- What needs to be added or eliminated to the project's objectives, activities, or resources?
- What efforts need to be made to overcome barriers?

Impact

- What is the intended impact of activities on participants?
- How has the project actually impacted participants?
- In what ways has the project impacted participants that were not intended?
- What factors have led to the intended as well as the unintended impact?
- How has the project impacted the organization and the community?

Strategy

- What strategies are being used to address the condition?
- What has been postponed or eliminated from the strategy, and why?
- What factors contribute to the effectiveness of the project's strategy?
- What inhibits its effectiveness?
- What is missing from the strategy?
- What resources need to be redirected or added to support the strategy?

WORKSHEET C

Step 1: Focus the Evaluation

Example: St. Paul's Project: "Hospitality for Discipleship"

Subject	Purpose	Audience	Evaluation Questions	Why is this question important?
Mentoring relationships	Gauge quality of mentoring relationships	Mentors, committee members	What are the ways mentors establish relationships with newcomers?	Committee members and mentors want to identify some of the best practices used by mentors
			What do newcomers most value about the mentoring relationship?	
			What is least effective for them?	

Subject	Purpose	Audience	Evaluation Questions	Why is this question important?
	Understand impact on newcomers	Mentors, committee members	What do newcomers learn about the parish? What activities do they become involved in? Why? If they don't become involved, why not? What is important to newcomers in the mentoring program?	Leaders, committee members, and mentors want to know what difference the program makes in people's participation levels in the parish

amount of data to collect. There is always the temptation to collect a great deal of data, but if the questions are not clearly defined prior to collecting information, evaluators will have a difficult time determining what to do with the data.

EVALUATORS AND EVALUATION TEAMS

The final task in focusing the evaluation is for project leaders to identify a person to lead the evaluation. A lead evaluator takes responsibility for executing steps 2, 3, 4, and 5: completing the evaluation design, identifying talented people to assist in the evaluation, and overseeing its execution and completion. The lead evaluator can certainly be a person from the project or organization, so long as they can be a sympathetic critic.

The most important characteristic of a lead evaluator is a capacity to discern and interpret the evaluation findings—step 4. Because we often think of evaluation more narrowly as collecting data, we think of evaluators who are experts in creating valid surveys. A lead evaluator is not necessarily required to have expertise in step 3, data collection methods, though experience can certainly help them with the task. More importantly, however, is what happens with the data after it is collected. A good lead evaluator is someone who can study the "raw data" that comes from evaluation forms and turn it into knowledge people can understand and use. And that transformation of data into knowledge is what discernment and interpretation are all about. Lead evaluators are also people who value the kind of learning generated through an evaluation and who can guide the evaluation process as a form of collaborative inquiry.

Identifying a lead evaluator does not preclude a committee on evaluation or an evaluation team; however, in cases where a group of people are involved in the evaluation, it is still helpful to identify a leader. Most projects, particularly large-scale efforts, benefit from the formation of an evaluation team—a group of people who can gather information, interpret it, and prepare reports. Evaluation teams who are engaged in collaborative inquiry together can create opportunities for reflection and conversation about what they are learning. Team members may include people from the project or organization, as well as consultants or data collection experts outside the project. Team members might also include people who have access to the data, such as a database manager. The diagram below describes various configurations of lead evaluators and evaluation teams.

Examples of Evaluation Teams

Committee Members
LE = lead evaluation, E = evaluators

Camp Longwood LE = director E = assistant director and 　a secretary	**St. Paul's Church** LE = committee chair E = committee members
First Plymouth Church LE = committee member E = 2 committee members 　2 people from other 　　communities 　a local college professor 　2 pastors	**Emmaus Seminary** LE = academic dean E = 2 faculty members 　director of external 　　relations 　database manager 　student in the Doctor 　　of Ministry program

Characteristics of Effective Evaluators

- Capacity to discern and interpret evaluation findings.
- Interest in the project's value.
- Respect from the evaluation's primary audience.
- Sufficient time to do the work.
- Enthusiasm for learning, collaborative style, and a good listener.
- Honesty and integrity.
- Ability to communicate and facilitate learning among the primary audiences.

Is it ever necessary to use an expert in evaluation or data collection methods? Of course it is. In some cases it might be impossible for an organization to get the evaluation done without employing outside help; or the sensitivity of the evaluation might preclude staff involvement. Certainly people with expertise in particular evaluation methods can be invited to serve on an evaluation team. For example, a committee might need someone who knows how to design a survey form and calculate the quantitative responses; another group may have little experience in conducting interviews and seek out help for how to write questions, conduct an interview, and interpret the data. Where can you find such people? Start with the people in the organization; if no one is available with the talents you need, look to other organizations similar to your own. If you cannot find someone in your immediate vicinity, contact a local school or university—educators use a variety of evaluation and research methods, as do sociologists, ethnographers, and psychologists, and may be helpful resources or consultants.

The first step in evaluation involves clarification of four issues defined in step 1: subject, audiences, purposes, and personnel. Answers to the questions outlined in step 1 are not always immediately self-evident, and that is why focusing takes time. Project leaders can begin by creating a process in which project stakeholders can have input in the early stages of evaluation planning. In some cases, project leaders may need authorization and approval to move forward with an evaluation. In any event, evaluations will be useful if there is agreement about the focus of the evaluation at the earliest phase.

Focusing the Evaluation

- What is being evaluated?
- For what purpose?
- Who will learn and benefit from the evaluation?
- What are the key questions to be explored?
- Who will conduct the evaluation?

Step 2
Create an Evaluation Design

Focus

Design ◀

Collect Data

Analyze & Interpret

Report

Revise Rationale

- State purposes, audiences, and key questions.
- Describe the data-collection activities and the persons responsible for the work.
- Determine type of reports necessary for various audiences.
- Develop a schedule for evaluation activities and preparation of reports.
- Establish an evaluation budget.

The second step is to create an evaluation design. As mentioned previously, evaluation constitutes a project activity so that the various components—tasks, resources, schedule, and results—need to be determined at the outset. An evaluation design consists of three major parts: (1) the purpose, audience, and key questions of the evaluation (defined in step 1); (2) the evaluation activities, which includes gathering data, interpreting information, and preparing reports; and (3) a schedule and budget.

Step 2 is collaborative work among project leaders and evaluators: the design may go through several drafts before a final plan is agreed upon. The lead evaluator's work begins here. The first part of the evaluation design has been defined by project leaders; the evaluator's work is to describe how the key questions will be answered and how the information will be shared. At the completion of step 2, project leaders, along with the evaluators, will have a plan that defines the expectations and strategy for the evaluation.

DESCRIBE DATA COLLECTION ACTIVITIES

In order to answer the key questions, evaluators must identify, first, sources of answers, and, second, ways to gather information from these sources. A good rule to follow is to build evaluation into project activities, not onto them. Evaluators may consider whether answers to some of the evaluation questions are already provided within the project itself. Start with a data inventory that identifies all the ways by which the project is already collecting data. For example, application forms are an easy way to collect demographic information; applicants may also be asked open-ended questions in order to determine their attitudes or knowledge about a topic prior to participating in the program. Camp Longwood wants to understand how applicants find out about the camp and who encouraged them to attend; a question on the application form can provide evaluators with this information in an efficient way. If evaluators can glean information from existing documents or activities, they can eliminate unnecessary repetition. Once existing sources of information are identified, evaluators can determine what evaluation instruments need to be created.

Gathering Information

- What information is needed to answer the evaluation questions?
- Who has the information?

There are several methods evaluators can choose from to gather information. Step 3 describes in detail five evaluation methods; evaluators who are unfamiliar with these methods may want to review the description of each method, along with the strengths and weaknesses, to determine which method is best for the kind of information they seek. As the evaluation activities are defined, the lead evaluator will need to consider who will be responsible for the task of designing and executing the method. Teams of evaluators will require clear directions regarding each person's tasks and a schedule for when their work is to be completed.

DEVELOP A SCHEDULE FOR EVALUATION ACTIVITIES

A schedule for evaluation activities can be determined according to the project's schedule of activities. Data gathering may occur at several points during the course of a project: before activities begin (e.g., application forms, pretests, interviews); during the project (e.g., observations of activities, written tests or surveys after an event, evaluators' journal entries during activities, or interviews); at the completion of a project (e.g., exit interviews, focus groups, or surveys); or at some point in the future after the project has been completed. When scheduling evaluation activities, evaluators should include time for gathering data, analyzing and interpreting the information, and preparing evaluation reports—steps 3, 4 and 5. Worksheet D illustrates five elements of Emmaus Seminary's evaluation design.

Evaluation Methods

- analysis of project materials
- direct observation
- interviews and focus groups
- surveys and questionnaires
- tests

DEVELOP A PLAN FOR REPORTING TO THE EVALUATION'S AUDIENCES

It is also important to include in the evaluation design a plan for how each audience will receive information from the evaluation, in what form, and according to the schedule appropriate to the needs of each audience. Evaluators may be required to prepare written reports or make oral presentations (see step 5). If the evaluation is to serve as a means for learning, the design should include times and formats for discussing evaluation findings. For example, in mapping out the audiences and reports, be mindful of when different audiences need to receive information (perhaps at the spring board meeting, or before the next planning and budget cycle), and an effective way to share the information.

Evaluation Activities and Reporting

- When do the various audiences need to receive information from the evaluation?
- What implication does the reporting schedule have for the evaluation activities and schedule?
- When do the evaluation activities need to occur?
- What can occur prior to, during, and after project activities?

WORKSHEET D
Step 2: Evalaution Design
Example: Emmaus Seminary: Service in and for the Community

Purpose/ Questions	Data Sources	Methods	Person Responsible	Schedule
Determine results and quality of events	Neighbors	Ask attendees to fill out a guest card at each event; ask for name, address, and reason for attending	Joann	Fall festival, October 3 Spring concert, April 4
How effective are festival and spring concerts at attracting people from the neighborhood?		Track numbers at each event; guest cards will track repeat visits		
How many people attended each event and what can their attendance be attrobuted to?				

Purpose/ Questions	Data Sources	Methods	Person Responsible	Schedule
Identify impact of faculty research on local organizations and faculty	Leaders of local organizations	Interview five leaders of local	Peter	Six months after start-up of faculty involvement in project
	Committee members of local projects	Interview 15 committee members		
In what ways are local organizations utilizing faculty research?	Faculty members	Interview participating faculty		Once a year for three years
How has involvement in the local community impacted faculty teaching and research?				
What are some unintended ways organizations and faculty have been impacted?				

Purpose/ Questions	Data Sources	Methods	Person Responsible	Schedule
Analyze project strategy	Information from evaluation of events and impact on organizations and faculty	Analyze all written materials and evaluations	External evaluator	Final year of project
To what extent does hosting events and supporting involvement in local organizations heighten our public presence in the community?	Analysis of other seminaries' efforts to increase public presence	Collect information from other seminaries; interview 10 presidents		
What inhibits the community's involvement in seminary events?		Interview project leaders and board members		
What are the drawbacks to faculty working on local projects?				
Are there other initiatives to add to the project?				

WORKSHEET E
Audiences and Evaluations Reports
Example: St. Paul's "Hospitality for Discipleship" Project

Audiences	Type of Report	Schedule for Reporting
Quality of mentoring relationships: Committee members	Summary of interviews conducted with newcomers compiled into a brief report	Every six months over the first 18 months of the project
Quality of mentoring relationships: Mentors	Report from interviews and a debriefing meeting with committee members	After 12 and 18 months
Impact on newcomers: Committee members and mentors	Summary of interviews and focus groups with newcomers	18 months after initiation of the program
Impact on newcomers: Parish board	A final report prepared by committee members and presented to the board, including description of effective mentoring relationships and the impact on newcomers; also includes areas of weakness and suggestions for improvement	Parish board meeting following the first 18-month phase of the project

Worksheet E provides an example of St. Paul's reporting activities and schedule for each audience.

ESTABLISH AN EVALUATION BUDGET

The final step in preparing an evaluation is to determine how much the evaluation will cost. As evaluation activities are defined, the cost for personnel, time, and materials will become clearer. The cost of an evaluation can vary in terms of the size of the project and the scope of the evaluation, particularly when outside experts are hired. Many evaluation experts suggest that 3 to 5 percent of the project budget be dedicated to evaluation. It is obviously difficult to advise all organizations to follow these figures absolutely; organizations and projects vary to such a large degree, such a guideline might be meaningless in some situations. Based on the experience of evaluation experts, however, it is a good place to start. Evaluators can ask: if we are spending more than 5 percent on evaluation, is that too much? Or if we are spending less than 3 percent, is that too little? The primary costs of an evaluation are usually consultant fees and materials; at times, travel costs may be involved. Worksheet F is an example of the categories that make up an evaluation budget.

Determining the Cost of the Evaluation

- Whose time will be needed to conduct the evaluation?
- Are external consultants needed?
- Will travel be involved?
- What materials will need to be produced (e.g., interview guides, surveys)?
- What office support may be required (e.g., database entry, collation of materials, mailings)?

Creating an evaluation design requires thoughtful consideration by project leaders and evaluators. The design provides a road map for what the evaluation will do; it serves as a commitment between organizational leaders, project leaders and staff, and evaluators. The quality of the evaluation will largely rest on how concrete the design is; but a detailed design does not imply a rigid plan. Similar to project activities, the evaluation design needs

WORKSHEET F
Evaluation Budget

Budget Category:	Year 1	Year 2	Year 3	Total
Time				
Consultants				
Travel				
Office supplies				
—Telephone				
—Photocopies				
—Mail				
TOTAL				

to be flexible and responsive to the project; adjustments can be made to the evaluation design as the work unfolds. The process of designing an evaluation is a team effort. The design should be the initial process of collaboration between project leaders and stakeholders: it is an opportunity for leaders to clarify the purposes and tasks of evaluation, as well as create ownership and enthusiasm around the evaluation for its stakeholders.

Critiquing the Evaluation Design

- What are the constraints that may inhibit the execution of the evaluation?
- Is the evaluation feasible in terms of resources—people, time, and expense?
- What are the limits to the evaluation? What questions will not be answered?

After the first draft of an evaluation design, evaluators and project leaders may determine that the evaluation is too ambitious, or does not address the right issues, involve the right people, or ask the right questions. It may be unrealistic given the organization's time and resources. It is helpful to step back from the design and critique it; a trusted colleague or expert may be asked to review the evaluation design for its feasibility and potential problems. Again, if the information from the evaluation is to be useful, the plan must be reasonable.

Characteristics of Good Evaluation Design

- a collaborative exercise on the part of project leaders, stakeholders, and evaluators
- firm, clear, and specific, yet flexible
- realistic about what can be accomplished in the evaluation
- a commitment to making a good project better

Step 3
Collect and Record Data

Focus

Design

Collect
Data ◀

Analyze &
Interpret

Report

Revise
Rationale

- Gather information through written materials, direct observation, interviews, surveys, and tests.
- Create a written narrative as the project evaluation unfolds.

At least five methods may be used to gather information in evaluations— analysis of written materials, direct observation, interviews, surveys and questionnaires, and tests. Each method is best suited for gathering particular kinds of information. This chapter briefly describes each method along with its strengths and weaknesses; evaluators who need more information are encouraged to check the resources listed in the bibliography. At times, an evaluation can be strengthened by seeking assistance from an expert in a particular research or evaluation method; evaluators can ask that an expert review methods prior to data collection, or facilitate the data collection and preliminary analysis.

Most evaluations use multiple approaches to gather information. Methods can be either quantitative or qualitative: quantitative methods are used to count and measure, and qualitative methods are used to describe. It is important to select data-collection methods that audiences will perceive as accurate, fair, and credible. There is always a temptation in collecting too much information; this often happens when evaluators begin with methods, rather than questions. A common mantra among evaluation experts is that evaluators should collect only the information that is going to be used, and use all the information that is collected. The place to begin, then, is with the evaluation's key questions. If information cannot be used to answer a question in the evaluation, it is probably not necessary.

Tips on Evaluation Methods

- Evaluation questions should guide data collection.
- Build data collection into project activities, not onto them.
- Determine how evaluation findings will be used before collecting information.
- Be sure evaluation methods are credible with the evaluation's audiences.
- Use multiple methods, both qualitative and quantitative.
- When appropriate, consult someone with expertise in a particular evaluation method.

WRITTEN MATERIALS

Evaluators will usually begin by examining the project's written materials and records. Project materials shed light on a project's identity, history, relationship to the organization, and the project's place in the organization's strategic plan. Documents to be analyzed may include mission statements, organizational charts, annual reports, activity schedules, funding proposals, participant records, promotional literature, and meeting minutes. In addition, project participants often create written materials that evaluators might find useful: applications, evaluation forms, journals, or essays.

Analyzing project materials will help evaluators understand the project's identity, its place in the sponsoring organization's strategy, and how the project has changed over time. Evaluators might compare official statements with information they gather from interviews or surveys to see how participants understand the project compared with how it represents itself. When reading through materials, evaluators should be guided by a set of questions or themes; they will want to look for specific information. For example, evaluators on Emmaus Seminary's project reviewed 10 years of seminary documents to learn what ways the seminary was involved in the local community in the past. Evaluators reviewed strategic plans, board minutes, and faculty research grant proposals. Analyzing the seminary's materials was helpful in setting the current project in the context of the seminary's history and mission.

Analyzing written materials is generally an inexpensive evaluation method. Evaluators will want to remember that documents have a particular historical context and were written for particular audiences, so information should not be taken out of context. Furthermore, written materials seldom provide all the information that is needed to answer an evaluation question. Therefore, information gleaned from project materials probably needs to be compared with information gathered from participants.

Analyzing Written Materials

- What documents should be read and analyzed?
- How are project goals described?
- What themes can be tracked through project documents?
- What questions are raised by the materials?

DIRECT OBSERVATION

Direct observation is a method that is often used in a project but is overlooked as an evaluation method. Its main purpose is to describe the physical setting of a project, its activities and events, as well as people's behaviors, including nonverbal communication, emotions, and expressions. For example, in evaluating the effectiveness of each noontime session, members at First Plymouth will observe the interactions between speakers and participants.

Observers can be people inside or outside the project. Insiders, for example, can be project staff who are already observing and participating in project activities. They can be invited to record their observations for purposes of the evaluation. The advantage of inside observers is that they can often see and hear important nuances and meanings that outsiders may fail to understand. Members of First Plymouth's adult education committee are suitable observers: they can look for ways that people are engaging the speaker and ideas as well as some barriers that might be inhibiting their learning. Outside observers—people not familiar with the project or organization—also bring a unique perspective because they often see and hear aspects of an activity or event that go unnoticed by insiders.

In both cases, observers need direction. Like the analyst of materials, observers need a set of questions to guide their observation. Obviously, they cannot see everything. They require direction: what they are to observe, the number of times an event or activity is to be observed, and a set of questions to answer. For example, two First Plymouth committee members will observe each noontime event and take note of the teaching styles of each presenter, and the interest and participation of attendees. During or after the observation, observers will need to record what they saw; a record is necessary in order to analyze and interpret the information in step 4. Observers may want to take notes, though this can be disruptive in some situations; they may write and tape their findings afterwards, but they should not wait too long. Again, observers should record their observations in relationship to the questions guiding their observation. First Plymouth committee members have decided to rotate as observers so they can compile a variety of observations; they will summarize their notes after each session, share the summaries in committee meetings, and compare their findings.

Direct Observation

- What evaluation questions can be answered through direct observation?
- Who might be able to serve as an observer from the project staff or organization?
- What activities or events might require a perspective from outside the organization?
- What questions will guide the observation?
- How will observers record their observation?
- To whom will they report their findings, how, and by when?

Direct observation is relatively easy and inexpensive, especially when project staff members or other volunteers are observers. Observations can help to understand project activities as they occur and provide an immediate basis for making changes in subsequent activities. Observations might be of limited value if evaluators rely on a single observer or observe a single event; the observation may be overly subjective, impressionistic, or skewed by a single person's observation or by observing only one event. Multiple observations are needed, and other methods are necessary to corroborate and verify the information gathered through observation. In addition, an observer is not an invisible or passive presence, so observers need to be aware of how they affect participants and an activity. In particular, confidentiality and cultural norms should be taken into consideration when conducting an observation.

INTERVIEWS

Interviews are a popular method in evaluation because they serve many purposes. Interviews allow evaluators to ask people to explain their attitudes, feelings, and interpretations of events, aspects of their experience that are not always observable. Interviews can expand upon, and sometimes correct, information gathered through observation; they offer an opportunity to compare what people do with what they say. Evaluators have the opportunity to hear individual stories, diverse perspectives, and minority voices.

Generally not all project participants can or need to be interviewed, though there may be times and reasons for interviewing everyone. Time constraints often prohibit a large number of interviews, but it is also important to remember that interviewing all the people does not make the information more reliable or valid. Before evaluators commit to interviews, it is important to define which evaluation questions are best answered through interviews and who needs to be interviewed in order to answer the questions. Interviewees should represent diversity within the project as well as distinct subgroups. People who are invited to participate in an interview should be informed of the interview method (in person or via the telephone), the amount of time involved, and how the information will be recorded and used.

Types of Interviews

- Unstructured, informal interviews are conversations in which interviewers allow information to emerge from their interaction with the respondent.
- Structured interviews with open-ended responses involve the use of an interview guide by an interviewer. Interviewers can outline a set of topics, themes, and questions in advance to cover during the interview, or interviewers can create a set of questions that all interviewees will be asked in the same order.
- Closed-structured interviews involve asking questions determined in advance, and asking respondents to choose from a set of fixed responses. These types of interviews are like surveys, and are often used in opinion polls.
- Focus groups are discussion groups involving between five and fifteen people. Predetermined questions and issues invite interaction and exchange among participants, but not necessarily agreement.

Evaluators of Camp Longwood's marketing project will conduct 15 telephone interviews with pastors who received the camp's new promotional kit. Evaluators will ask several questions, including:

1. What materials from the recruitment kit did you use?
2. What did you find helpful about the materials? What materials did you not use or find helpful? Why?
3. How many young people from your congregation attended camp? Did you recruit for the camp? What kind of follow-up did you provide when the children returned?
4. Did any other adults in the congregation recruit and support young people to attend the Camp? If so, who recruited or supported the young people and how?

Interviews often give evaluators substantial amounts of information with lots of details. Interviews are interpersonal encounters that affect both the interviewer and the respondent. In many cases, the interviewee is telling about their personal experience that can involve moments of joy as well as disappointment. Interviewers are entrusted with important information about people's lives, and will need to respect and honor a person's individual experience. Interviewers themselves can be deeply moved by the stories they hear and attracted to the most compelling reports; over the course of the interviews, they will need to balance the many and varied stories they hear, giving credence to all voices and experiences.

In many cases not all the information interviewers receive is pertinent or valid to the evaluation. In fact, interviewers may need to sort through some of the motives behind some answers. Individuals may, for example, tell the interviewer what he or she believes they want to hear or participants might conceal their feelings or interpretations to protect the project. In contrast, persons may want to gossip or sabotage the project by telling evaluators details that are beyond the scope of the evaluation. In some cases, interviewees may give inaccurate factual information. Evaluators will want to guide interviewees by asking questions and probing for information that will aid the evaluation and the project. As is the case with direct observations, evaluators may also need to verify or substantiate information through other sources.

Designing Interviews

- What answers to evaluation questions can be gathered through interviews?
- Who will be interviewed? How many interviews need to be conducted in order to glean sufficient and reliable information?
- Will interviews be in person or on the telephone?
- What questions will be asked in the interview?

SURVEYS

Surveys are also a commonly used evaluation method because of the particular kinds of information that can be gathered. In general, surveys are used to gather quantitative information such as demographics, and measurement and comparisons of attitudes, knowledge, or beliefs. Surveys are the most efficient means for collecting information from a large group of people. Surveys also help to gather responses to sensitive questions that participants may not feel comfortable answering in an interview. Respondents require clear instructions in how to answer questions.

Types of Survey Questions

- Closed-ended surveys state questions and offer respondents a set of predetermined answers. The answers can be as simple as yes or no, or involve multiple choice, usually up to five possible responses. Because closed-ended questions and answers do not explain why someone answered as they did, two other types of questions can be used in closed-ended surveys.
- Contingency questions follow closed-ended questions to invite further explanation (e.g., "If yes, why?").
- Scaled or continuum questions offer a range of responses between two end points, such as "strongly agree" and "strongly disagree." Continuum questions usually give four to five options, which allow respondents to qualify their opinions between two end points.
- Open-ended questions allow respondents to create their own answers to a question.

Examples of Survey Questions
from First Plymouth's Survey of Participants

Closed-ended:
How many interfaith dialogue events did you attend? (Check one.)
_____ 1-2 _____ 3-4 _____ 5-6

Contingency:
Did the events provide substantive information about other religions?
_____ Yes _____ No

If yes, what information did you gain? If no, what information did you hope would be presented?

Multiple Choice:
Do you think First Plymouth should continue interfaith dialogue events in the future?

_____ Yes, keep the format the same

_____ Yes, but change the format

_____ No, the format is causing conflict

_____ No, interfaith dialogue is not part of our mission

Scaled continuum: 1 = strongly disagree; 10 = strongly agree

I learned a great deal about other religions.
1   2   3   4   5   6   7   8   9   10

I enjoyed meeting people from other communities.
1   2   3   4   5   6   7   8   9   10

Interfaith dialogue can promote the city's common good.
1   2   3   4   5   6   7   8   9   10

Open-ended: What are some insights you gained about your Christian faith by attending interfaith dialogues?

Surveys are helpful instruments to gather people's attitudes and impressions, but they are limited in terms of allowing evaluators to see and understand behavior. They can be costly depending on how they are conducted (e.g., direct mail or employing outside survey companies). Using a project Web site can be a cost-saving way to survey people.

Surveys can be time-consuming to answer, depending upon the number and length of questions; they can also be time-consuming for evaluators to analyze. In some instances, surveys can be less effective with some groups than, say, interviews; children, for example, or elderly members of a community may have difficulty filling out a survey. For all these reasons, evaluators should use surveys on a limited basis; they should be easy for participants to use and not too difficult for evaluators to analyze.

Using Surveys

- What evaluation questions will be answered through a survey?
- Who will be surveyed—all participants or a sample?
- How many people need to be surveyed in order to yield reliable results?
- Do stakeholders believe the sample is reliable?

TESTS

Tests are helpful to gather information about what people know regarding a set of concepts or issues. Tests may be used prior to project activities to provide a baseline of information about what a target population knows; the information can be used to refine activities and insure that program goals are reached. Posttests can be used to determine what participants have learned at the conclusion of activities or the project. For example, evaluators at First Plymouth want to understand what congregants know about other religious communities in Plymouth prior to adult education classes. They design a form that asks people to explain what they know about other communities, their basic beliefs, worship traditions, and location, in the city of Plymouth. The form will be administered prior to the adult education classes and again at the end; the information will allow evaluators to compare participants' knowledge before and after the session. It can also be used by the teacher as a basis for preparing course materials. A test may be inappropriate in some groups, as they can cause fear and anxiety. It is also important to remember that tests do not reflect attitudes, impressions, or behaviors.

Utilizing Tests

- What information can be gathered through a pre- or posttest?
- Who should be tested?

RECORDING INFORMATION

As evaluators use each of these methods, they will need to develop efficient means of recording information, as well as impressions, so they are not lost. If evaluators wait to write their observations or to review interview notes, they run the risk of forgetting what they saw or heard, and may lose some of their initial impressions. Generally, evaluators should review data and complete notes as soon as possible. The way each evaluator records information will vary. Some evaluators record notes, others may need a set of questions to answer, and others may want to keep a journal. How evaluators record and keep information is largely a matter of personal style. The next step, the analysis and interpretation of the data, will be affected by how well the evaluator collects, records, and stores information.

Summary of Methods Table

Method	Types of Information	Strengths	Limitations
Written materials	Allows evaluators to understand how a project is understood by those who developed it; can be compared with what people understand the project to be about. Also enables assessment of what participants are able to do or what they have to say.	Inexpensive, offers historical and contextual understanding of the project	Materials are written with particular audiences in mind, so not all the information about a project will be available.
Direct observation	Description of physical setting, nonverbal communication, and behaviors	Easy and inexpensive	Subjective, impressionistic
Interviews	Captures attitudes, feelings, and interpretations; allows comparison of explanations with behavior	Individual stories emerge as well as general patterns	Subjective, feelings and ideas may be concealed or distorted
Surveys	Can be used to gather quantitative information; effective for measuring and comparing attitudes or knowledge of large groups of people	Can be used to gain answers to sensitive questions; supplies quantitative and qualitative information	Can be time consuming to answer; and time consuming and costly to analyze
Tests	Can be used to gather information about what people know	Focuses on knowledge	Does not capture attitudes, impressions, or behaviors

Step 4
Analyze and
Interpret Information

Focus

Design

Collect
Data

Analyze &
Interpret

Report

Revise
Rationale

- Compose an accurate picture of the evaluation's subject.
- Interpret the meaning of evaluation findings.

In step 4, evaluators analyze and interpret data collected from project materials, observations, interviews, surveys, and tests. "Raw data" is turned into information and knowledge that others learn from and use. Step 4 consists of two main tasks. First, evaluators identify the key findings by calculating quantities, analyzing qualitative data for themes and patterns, selecting important information, and comparing findings. The first task results in an accurate picture of the evaluation's subject. A second task involves interpreting the meaning of the findings: offering explanations, examining contexts and influential factors, identifying contradictions and missing pieces, highlighting values and motivations, and offering, from the evaluator's point of view, questions and recommendations for project leaders to consider. Together, these two tasks produce the key evaluation findings.

Of course, step 4 is not an isolated activity; evaluators classify, organize, and interpret data throughout step 3. But step 4 is a distinct process, because at some point, evaluators must stop gathering data and begin to think, synthesize, and make judgments. Remember that good evaluations are not measured by the sheer amount of data accumulated; rather, good evaluation findings rest on the quality of information that evaluators and project leaders can use for the evaluation's purposes.

Step 4 is not only a distinct activity, but it requires the skill and gift of discernment. At this point in the evaluation process the evaluator becomes a discerning critic and judge. Discernment in evaluation means that evaluators compile an accurate description of the situation, including the subject's salient features as well as those that are hidden, obscure, and absent. This requires time for reflection and consideration of all the data. Discernment demands that evaluators have an open mind in order that the multitude of voices and perspectives can be heard and understood. Some findings will come immediately; others are more opaque, perhaps confusing, and even contradictory. Discernment, then, is a matter of both perception and judgment; at this point, evaluators are more like a discerning literary or wine critic than an accountant or pollster.

ACCURATELY DESCRIBE THE SUBJECT BASED ON EVALUATION DATA

Describe the Evaluation's Subject

- Review evaluation questions.
- Calculate quantitative information.
- Analyze qualitative data for common themes and patterns.
- Compare findings from various methods.
- Compose an accurate picture of the subject.

Before evaluators read, sort, and analyze the interviews or surveys or tests, it is helpful to look back at steps 1 and 2 and recall the purposes of the evaluation, its main audiences, and the key questions the evaluation seeks to answer. The questions and concerns of the audiences should inform the evaluator's work in step 4. Of course, evaluators are not looking for information that audiences want to hear; rather, they want to offer audiences information that will shed light on their questions, even if the responses are not exactly what was hoped for.

Evaluators first sort data to be analyzed through quantitative and qualitative analysis. Quantitative analysis yields information in the form of numbers: statistics such as percentages and averages. Because statistics carry significant weight in our culture, evaluators will want to insure that statistical findings should be presented in a way that does not distort their meaning. Statistics may require explanation as well as qualification. Evaluators can help audiences understand the numbers in their proper context in order to avoid inaccurate generalizations or conclusions.

Quantitative Analysis

- Calculate numerical findings into statistics.
- What insights do the findings yield?
- Do they make sense? Why or why not?
- What are some possible explanations for surprises or distortions?
- How do these findings relate to the evaluation questions?
- What information is missing?

Qualitative analysis requires evaluators to use a different set of skills from statistical analysis. In qualitative analysis, evaluators are searching through responses to open-ended questions from interviews, surveys, tests, and observers' notes and notes from written materials to find common themes and stories. The first task is to find similarities and patterns that appear frequently. The next step is to compare patterns across various subgroups of people to see what broad patterns can be summarized into main themes. Counting the times an idea or issue is mentioned is an efficient way to determine how important something is. Qualitative data also contain quotes, anecdotes, or stories that can be used to illuminate the major findings. It is important to remember that the findings that emerge from qualitative analysis are more like a novel or movie than a still-life photograph: they contain the narratives of people's experience and capture the nonquantifiable aspects of experience and ideas. But evaluators will want to be cautious: one or two anecdotes can be so compelling that they dominate the evaluator's reading of the situation. The best stories must be placed alongside those that are not as pleasing and interesting.

Qualitative Analysis

- Read observation notes and open-ended answers from interviews, surveys, and tests.
- Categorize and code material.
- Make notes or lists of common ideas and themes.
- Consider what is distinctive and different from other findings.
- Note important narratives.
- Note discrepancies in people's experiences when compared together.
- Ask, What is missing?

Step 4. Analyze and Interpret Information

As evaluators glean information from quantitative and qualitative sources, they can begin to compare the two sets of findings. How do qualitative findings relate to the quantitative findings? What can be further claimed and confirmed when the information is combined? As evaluators draw together the insights from the quantitative and qualitative analysis, evaluation findings begin to emerge. The findings should provide an accurate reading of the subject. A comprehensive description of the project should allow audiences to understand the relationship between activities and resources and their results and impact. From such a description, audiences can begin to understand what is happening in the project. The next task helps them to understand why.

At the conclusion of the first year of events at Emmaus Seminary, evaluators analyze guest cards filled out by participants who attended the fall festival and spring concert. Findings include: 20 percent of the neighbors invited attended the fall festival, and 27 percent attended the spring concert; 15 percent of the people attended both; neighbors reported that they felt welcome at the seminary; many reported they knew little about what the seminary did; 60 percent reported interest in attending future events.

INTERPRET THE MEANING OF EVALUATION FINDINGS

The evaluator's next interpretive task is to help audiences understand the meaning of evaluation findings. In addition to the description of activities, resources, and impact, evaluators can help audiences see why certain activities yield particular results, and how various kinds of resources affect the quality of activities and their results. Evaluators can go beyond the immediate and obvious aspects of the project to illuminate what may be obstructed from view. They can examine contexts and distinguish between various factors that contribute to the quality of project results. Of course, some of these factors are internal to the project and organization, while some exist in the external environment but play a significant role in determining outcomes. Project leaders may be aware of these dynamics, but the evaluation can bring further insight and explanation to the range of factors influencing the project results and impact.

One interesting surprise emerged from Emmaus Seminary's evaluation. Evaluators and project leaders thought turnout to the events was low. When those who did not attend were asked why, many neighbors noted that a school play was scheduled for the same day. Low attendance, then, did not mean a lack of interest in seminary events, but a schedule conflict for some. Evaluators recommend that seminary officials check for major events in the community before setting the date for next year's festival.

Interpreting Findings

- Offer explanations for the key findings.
- Examine context and contributing factors.
- Identify surprises, contradictions, and missing pieces.
- Probe for guiding values and motives.
- Spell out some of the consequences if certain courses of action continue.
- Affirm successes and strengths.
- Raise questions and concerns and make recommendations.

Projects are full of surprises; sometimes fun and inspiring, other times disturbing and problematic. Evaluators can see factors that were not anticipated, and they can identify unexpected results as well as an unintended impact on project participants. The surprises can be gifts: they can open up new opportunities and ways of thinking about the project, but they can also be warning lights for project directors to avoid.

Evaluators may recognize contradictions in the project—claims that are made but not lived up to; people saying one thing but doing another. Furthermore, evaluators can name the missing pieces—materials that are needed, elements of activities that were overlooked, or a lack of time or talent in certain areas of the project. Discernment in evaluation also means identifying the values and motives that influence the people in the project. This includes the officially stated values of the project. It also includes the values people bring to the project—their reasons for participating, the values they hold in common with the project, and the values that may at times conflict with the project. The evaluation can shed some light on the reasons why people act and think in certain ways, and in a religious organization, people will be guided by religious values and beliefs.

When evaluators compose a comprehensive picture of the subject and interpret the meaning of the actions, beliefs, and dynamics, they have a unique vantage point on the project. They can sometimes see consequences of certain courses of action: if seminary leaders do not consider community events when scheduling activities, they will not maximize participation from their neighbors.

Step 4. Analyze and Interpret Information

Evaluators are not neutral observers or interpreters. They bring their own perspective and concerns to an evaluation. Evaluators should pose questions, raise concerns, affirm strengths, and point out weaknesses. They do so in their own voice. Yet discernment and interpretation are not solo enterprises, and evaluators should not be working alone at step 4. If evaluation is a collaborative enterprise, evaluators' perspectives are enriched and challenged by dialoguing with other evaluators and project leaders about the evaluation findings. Where there are differences in interpretation, these can be noted. The project will be strengthened, not threatened, by multiple perspectives and interpretations of what is taking place and why.

Evaluators should not shy away from claiming what they think or recommend. But how do evaluators make recommendations? I encourage evaluators to make many recommendations, realizing that it is up to project leaders to choose what they will do next in the project. Project leaders can be assisted in their deliberations about a project if they are offered creative suggestions that can help them think about what options are available and how they might approach them. In making recommendations, however, evaluators should stay within reasonable boundaries of the project and organization. Recommendations can be invitations to think more broadly or more strategically, so the tone and manner in which recommendations are presented matter. Often, thoughtful questions are helpful, as are sentences that stress action; for example, evaluators might ask, "In what ways might mentor training help define the relationship with newcomers?" or say, "Create a mentor training program that establishes clear guidelines for mentor relationships with newcomers."

Evaluators must speak the truth about a project, and that is not always so easy. At times, they may have to report difficult and disappointing news. At these times, thoughtful questions and creative recommendations can help project leaders see beyond the weaknesses to new possibilities. In other instances, the evaluation findings are quite positive and evaluators can help project leaders think about implications of their success for the project and organization. In all these cases, recommendations are a means to learning. If evaluators do their job well, project leaders will be better able to determine what should be done next.

Step 5
Report and
Disseminate Findings

Focus

Design

Collect
Data

Analyze &
Interpret

Report

Revise
Rationale

- Prepare written reports appropriate to various audiences.
- Create conversations around evaluation findings.

Evaluators share information in the form of written and oral reports for project leaders and the evaluation's audiences. Both types of communication can take place in informal settings (e.g., weekly or monthly staff debriefings or memos) and formal settings (e.g., press conferences or meetings to discuss evaluation reports). In step 2, project leaders and evaluators determined the kinds of reports and processes for sharing information with the primary audiences. Step 5 is the task of creating reports and hosting conversations; evaluators and project directors have a variety of ways to communicate evaluation findings through written materials and oral reports. Recall that primary audiences of the evaluation are distinguished from secondary audiences; each method discussed below could be used for either type of audience, though primary audiences usually receive information in the form of memos, reports, and summaries, and secondary audiences through publications.

PREPARE WRITTEN REPORTS APPROPRIATE
TO EACH AUDIENCE

Most evaluators take notes, prepare summaries, and write throughout an evaluation. Evaluators can provide project leaders information during a

Communicating Evaluation Findings

Written Reports

- memos
- evaluation reports
- executive summary
- reports to foundations
- publications (e.g., newsletters, articles, thesis projects)
- press release
- visual aids

Oral Reports

- periodic debriefings between evaluation team and project leaders
- staff meetings
- board meetings
- public presentations
- press conference

---

project through periodic memos. Short written documents that organize ideas will assist project leaders who want information in order to make adjustments during the course of the project; they will also assist evaluators at the time they prepare formal reports or publications.

Written reports provide a record of a project and organizational memory by providing future leaders with information and insights from the project. For all these reasons, it is important that evaluators write clear and concise reports, since many audiences will not be as close to the project as the evaluator and project staff. St. Paul's hospitality committee prepared a summary of evaluation findings for the parish board; they also discussed the findings at a board meeting and presented a plan for next steps in the project.

In some cases, evaluators will be called upon to write a formal evaluation report that draws together central elements of the project and evaluation. Formal evaluation reports can be used by project and organization leaders, as well as boards of directors and funders. A formal evaluation report contains a thorough description of the project's purposes, activities, resources, results and impact, along with thorough answers to the evaluation questions. When necessary, evaluators qualify their claims by describing the limits of the evaluation, and identifying information that cannot be explained or is missing. Evaluators should avoid far-reaching generalizations and inaccurate conclusions.

Elements of a Formal Report

- summary of the project goals, activities, resources, results, and rationale
- overview of the evaluation design
- answers to the key evaluation questions
- summary of evaluation findings
- insights resulting from the evaluators' analysis
- recommendations
- executive summary

Evaluators, or project leaders, may also prepare written reports for public audiences beyond the immediate primary audience. They may want to disseminate information about the project and evaluation findings to audiences who share an interest in the project's model and rationale. Project leaders or evaluators may consider publishing information in press releases, articles, books, or on a project Web site. Evaluators at First Plymouth prepared a report on the noontime lunch series for religious leaders of the city. They also provided information to a journalist from the local newspaper who was invited to write a story on the project.

Disseminating Evaluation Findings beyond the Project

- Who might benefit by learning from this project?
- What magazines, journals, or newsletters might be interested in publishing the findings?
- What information might those who are engaged in similar kinds of work want to know from the project?
- What aspects of the project's design are replicable?
- How do the evaluation findings corroborate other research findings?
- What is distinctive about the project?

CREATE CONVERSATIONS
AROUND EVALUATION FINDINGS

Evaluators, as well as project leaders, can create opportunities for conversation about evaluation findings. For example, in addition to evaluator's memos to project leaders, periodic meetings between evaluators and project leaders or staff, or organizational leaders, can be formative for the project. It can also be an opportunity for evaluators to ask for guidance or clarification before continuing with the evaluation. At important points in the project, meetings with board members, accrediting-agency officials, or foundation directors will be scheduled. Written reports can provide a basis to engage these audiences in conversation about evaluation's findings and the project. Some projects may have opportunity to host a press conference or public presentation. In all these situations, project leaders can draw on evaluation findings to describe the project and its rationale. For example, after two years of using the recruitment kit, Camp Longwood leaders invited denominational officials to a one-day meeting to discuss the camp's outreach to congregations and congregations' response. Emmaus Seminary sponsored a lecture series for the community that invited faculty to present their research and to reflect on its impact for their understanding of the community.

The communication of evaluation findings is an essential step in helping audiences to learn from the project's work. Project and institutional leaders can build interest and support by inviting audiences to reflect carefully on evaluation findings. They create a community of learners around the project by offering clear and reliable information. Most importantly, they can provide opportunities for people to examine and critique the project's rationale. In this way, leaders create collaborative inquiry that engages the project and its rationale. Projects are strengthened when leaders develop a strategy for creating conversation among a variety of people who can bring multiple perspectives to the work. Good projects have many stakeholders who care about the issues and people involved in a project: sharing evaluation findings is one way of building commitment to the work and sustaining the effort into the future.

Step 6

Revise the Project's Rationale

Focus

Design

Collect Data

Analyze & Interpret

Report

Revise Rationale

◄

- Make improvements to the project design.
- Restate the project's rationale.
- Incorporate insights into future work.
- Make changes in the evaluation design for the next phase of evaluation.

The final step in the evaluation process is the responsibility of project and organization leaders. In a formative evaluation, the findings emerge over the course of the project so that the leaders are continually using information to make improvements in project activities and resources. Summative evaluations give leaders the opportunity to build insights from past work into future efforts. In both cases, step 6 returns to the evaluation's purposes and how evaluation findings are to be used: to gauge quality of results? determine whether objectives and goals have been achieved? to improve activities and resources? to understand impact? to analyze strategy? And, how will project leaders take what is learned from evaluation and use it for the good of the project and the organization?

IMPROVE PROJECT DESIGN

Through evaluation, project leaders have gained a new, or at least a more realistic, perspective on the original project design. The evaluation provides information for leaders to revise aspects of the project design, strengthening some activities while abandoning others. Revisions in the project design

78

may include adjustments to schedules, new or enhanced activities, and changes in resources. Leaders at St. Paul's are more realistic about what mentors can achieve and newcomers are willing to do. They realize that if newcomers are going to become involved in the parish, they will need more time to explore the parish, and should not be rushed into making a decision about what activities to join. The hospitality committee has decided to offer study groups on particular topics and ministries so new members can learn more before they decide what to do in the parish.

RESTATE THE PROJECT'S RATIONALE

Revisions in the project design will require revisions to the project's rationale—the set of arguments that connect conditions, goals, resources, activities, results, and impact. Evaluation provides evidence that backs up a project's claims, making claims and arguments more credible, reliable, and accurate. It allows leaders to refine the rationale with greater precision and clarity. After sponsoring the noontime lunch series over the course of a year, First Plymouth's rationale can be restated in the following way:

a. Various models of interfaith dialogue are possible in the congregational setting.

b. First Plymouth employs a model of teaching by local religious leaders, emphasizing knowledge about the tradition and its community in Plymouth. Interfaith dialogue is enriched when local religious leaders provide basic information about their tradition; provide examples of the work their community does in the city; are warm and humorous; are able to talk about the strengths and weaknesses of their tradition.

c. Dialogues that take place during the noontime lunch break maximizes participation from the city's diverse residents; on average, 100 to 150 people attended each week.

d. First Plymouth's members gained knowledge about other faith communities through an adult education series about other faith communities. Participants were able to assist in the planning and marketing of the noontime series; they also were able to welcome and visit with people from other faiths. Furthermore, participation in worship services at synagogues, mosques, and churches give members greater appreciation of other worship styles and increases their sensitivity to what others experience when they come into First Plymouth.

e. The common good of the city is strengthened when members of religious communities learn about each other's traditions and practices, and meet one another face-to-face.

Reframing the Rationale

- What findings illuminate and enhance the program's rationale?
- What has been learned about the condition the project is addressing?
- What has been learned about the solutions attempted through the project?
- What has been learned that strengthens the project's claims and evidence about the condition and its solutions?
- In what ways did the activities and resources lead to desired project results and goals?
- How will activities and resources be modified in future work?
- What activities and resources might be needed in the future to sustain the work?

INCORPORATE INSIGHTS INTO FUTURE WORK

Evaluation is meant to strengthen a project, particularly if projects continue beyond the first plan and into a next phase; however, organizations are rarely engaged in just one project. The evaluation can provide information for other projects in the organization, in the present as well as in the future. What is learned from doing evaluation can also be incorporated into other projects and their evaluations. At Camp Longwood, project leaders have learned more about the congregations who send children to the camp; this information is important as they prepare a fund-raising strategy for next year.

MAKE CHANGES IN THE EVALUATION DESIGN

Evaluations have a beginning and an end. They cover a certain period in the course of a project. If project leaders determine the project will continue, they may want to return to step 1 and begin the process of designing an evaluation for the next phase of the project. This will require project leaders and evaluators to reconsider the subject, purposes, audiences, and questions for the evaluation. Evaluators may need to refine their methods and collect more or different information to confirm or fill gaps in evaluation findings. Evaluation is an important means by which an organization can learn, but it does not need to happen all the time. It happens best when project leaders are intentional about making evaluation a regular part of the organization's planning and execution of successful projects.

CONCLUSION

Key Points of Project Evaluation

Focus

Design

Collect
Data

Analyze &
Interpret

Report

Revise
Rationale

1. Focusing the evaluation means describing what will be evaluated, why, for whom, and by whom.
2. Creating an evaluation design includes detailing the subject, purpose, audiences, and key questions, along with data-collection methods, a schedule for reporting to audiences, and a budget.
3. Collecting and recording data can be accomplished through five methods: analysis of written materials, direct observation of activities and events, interviews, surveys, and tests.
4. Analyzing and interpreting data from these methods allows evaluators to create an accurate picture of the evaluation's subject, and interpret the meaning of evaluation findings.
5. Reporting and disseminating findings involves preparing written reports and hosting conversations for primary and secondary audiences.
6. Revising the rationale invites project leaders to use evaluation findings to strengthen the project's claims about conditions, activities, resources, results, and impact.

The purpose of my project—describing evaluation as collaborative inquiry and explaining six steps of evaluation—is to encourage religious organizations to create a culture of evaluation that enhances project goals and mission effectiveness. I do not mean to imply that religious organizations do not already have a culture of evaluation or employ effective evaluation strategies. In fact, comparing this book's approach to your organization's evaluation practices might be a helpful exercise. Ask yourself: What is our organization's philosophy of evaluation? What are our evaluation practices? What is helpful about our approach, and what is lacking? How can we improve our approach to evaluation?

I explained in this book's preface my capacity to do this project—my experience in coaching a variety of religious organizations in evaluation—and the condition I want to address: a lack of understanding about evaluation as a means for learning, which can strengthen an organization's accountability to its mission. My main activity has been writing this book, and the main resources I have used are time, a computer, a few books on evaluation, and conversations with many talented people. The result: a published book by the Alban Institute. But what about impact? What difference do I hope it makes in the thinking and practices of the reader?

First, I hope my project has helped to dispel some of the myths that surround evaluation. I hope I have convinced you what evaluation is *not*. It should not be extra work, but integral to what we do in a project; it should not be done solely by external consultants, but initiated and guided by organization and project leaders; and it is not something to think about at the end of a project, but rather as part of the initial phases of executing a project. Evaluation is not about putting a final grade on a project, or identifying the mistakes or failures; and it should certainly not be done for purposes of institutional maintenance.

I hope I have convinced the reader to think about evaluation in other ways. In particular, I hope one impact of this book is that project leaders see a more direct connection between project plans and evaluation designs. It is difficult to design an evaluation if there is not a coherent plan that spells out what the project is about; good plans lay the basis for a strong evaluation design, and evaluations provide ways of improving a good plan.

I hope another impact is greater understanding about the role of evaluation in organizational culture. When project staff are buried in the details of executing and implementing a project, evaluation can provide much-needed moments for reflection, for stepping back and taking stock of what is happening and why. Similarly for organizational leaders and boards: evaluation is more than reporting what happened, it is a catalyst for helping leaders discern what strategies to pursue and in what ways. Evaluation builds reflective practices within a project and an organization that can keep people thinking together about the conditions a project addresses, the various project components, and the rationale that holds it all together.

Step 6. Revise the Project's Rationale

I have only hinted at a rationale for why I think religious leaders should pay attention to project planning and evaluation. I think there is a deeper theological rationale for why we engage in planning and evaluation. In this book's conclusion, I want to consider how I think about these aspects of organizational life theologically, and why I think this approach is particularly apt for Christian leaders, organizations, and communities of faith.

Discerning and Prudent Stewards

Theological Perspectives on Planning and Evaluation

Consider the membership problem facing a prominent religious organization: in one community, membership drops from 120 to 64; in another, it declines from 200 to 20; and in yet another, declines from 100 to 10. Compare the success of another religious organization during roughly the same period of time: from its beginning, seven new communities are established in 20 years, another 321 in 34 years, followed by 200 in the next 50 years, and so on until 742 new communities are established, an average of 4.5 a year.

A modern observer may consider that this is the story of the decline and growth of U.S. congregations, but it is not. It reflects the decline and growth of an entirely different set of religious organizations in another time and place: the collapse of Benedictine monasteries in medieval Europe followed by the ascendance of the Cistercians. The Benedictine way of life had provided a primary form of religious organization in western Europe for nearly 500 years; but what was taken for granted as civilization's highest religious ideal began to fade and crumble under the weight of its own bureaucracy.

Monasticism itself, however, was not dead. The Cistercians came along claiming to restore *The Rule of St. Benedict*. Cistercian organizational design, according to medieval historian R. W. Southern, is "one of the masterpieces of medieval planning." The Cistercian "ideal" calls for simplicity, rational organization, and "energetic exploitation of resources." They designed a simple chain of command from top to bottom, uniform practice across all monasteries, and firm discipline carried out by monastic leaders rather than Europe's law courts. Such reforms in monastic life countered the problems besetting the Benedictines: a luxurious lifestyle, the disintegration of common life due to economic support through benefactors, and a general "spiritual malaise" due to the rote practice of monastic disciplines.

The Cistercians were certainly good planners, but there is more to their story. They were also good evaluators. One of the reforms they proposed was the General Chapter; the chapter had been proposed as a reform in earlier times in Benedictine monasteries but had not been implemented. The Cistercians retrieved and put into practice the annual General Chapter at which abbots were to hold each other accountable for what we would today call "mission effectiveness." Furthermore, they introduced a practice of annual visitation of each abbey by the abbot of the "mother" abbey, a further disciplinary practice to ensure the monks were living according to the Rule and the abbot was exercising effective leadership. The manual that set forth these practices is known as *Charta Caritatis*, the "Charter of Love." According to the Charter, charity is the basis for organizational discipline and is to be practiced "so that if they [monks] should at any time decline from their good resolution and the observance of their holy rule, which misfortune may God in his mercy avert, we may be able by our constant solicitude to bring them back to the religious life." The document did not spell out what the visiting abbots are supposed to do to evaluate the effectiveness of the abbey, but rather where they are to eat and sleep and who has jurisdiction over whom. So much for medieval evaluation designs.

Christians have created a variety of organizations to support the worship, ministry, and work of Christian communities over a long history. How have Christians maintained organizations so that the organization remains vital and creative in response to the conditions it faces? In what ways have religious organizations used planning and evaluation, in religiously informed ways, that contribute to the organization's strength and effectiveness? More specifically, how do Christians think about planning and evaluation in Christian terms?

I have come to think that the reason we engage in planning and evaluation comes from our tradition of Christian stewardship. I am particularly reminded of Jesus' story about the house built on rock: "That one is like a man building a house, who dug deeply and laid the foundation on rock; when a flood arose, the river burst against that house but could not shake it, because it had been well built" (Luke 6:48). What makes for a rock-solid foundation in religious organizations—the kind that any type of bad weather will not destroy? As elements of Christian stewardship, planning and evaluation are ways in which Christians care for, monitor, and ensure both a strong foundation and a descent house. Two ways in which stewards care for organizations are through the virtues of discernment and prudence. These three elements of the Christian life—stewardship, discernment, and prudence—are deeply connected to the health and vitality of religious organizations and the projects they pursue. They are virtues we look for in our leaders; certainly they are the essential qualities we want in a president or pastor. But they are also virtues to be nurtured by all who contribute to, participate in, and influence an organization's work. I would say they are part of the character or culture of a Christian organization—a way of being and doing work that is exhibited at all levels of an organization. The foundation of the house must be strong, but the people who build the house and the way they go about building it matter too.

Stewardship: A Virtue of Caring

Stewards in the Hebrew Scriptures and the New Testament have special responsibilities "over the house" (Gen. 43:19; 44:1-4); they are responsible for overseeing the master's table, servants, property, and finances. Stewards not only care for material goods but are entrusted with the care of the whole of creation (Gen. 1:28; 2:15). In the New Testament, stewards who are good managers are considered wise and prudent (Luke 12:35-48). They are responsible for the community's resources (1 Cor. 4:2) and called to be generous and gracious (1 John 3:17).

St. Paul extends the idea of stewardship beyond the care for material goods and calls upon Christians to be "servants of Christ and stewards of God's mysteries" (1 Cor. 4:1) and "good stewards of the manifold grace of God" through their service to one another (1 Pet. 4:10). To be stewards of God's mysteries and grace means we are entrusted with Christ's mission on earth. We are called upon to care for the tradition's resources—to keep alive the stories, practices, and ways of life that have faithfully sustained Christians for generations. Of all that stewards are called to do, we might say one of the greatest "mysteries" we are called upon to steward are organizations.

"Think of us in this way, as servants of Christ and stewards of God's mysteries."—1 Cor. 4:1

Why are organizations such great mysteries to us? A local radio advertisement for a contemporary church service invites those who are "spiritually sensitive and institutionally suspicious." Why do we feel suspicious of our institutions? Perhaps there are several reasons. As human creations, they can quickly become corrupt and corrupting. Who among us has not suffered or been disappointed at the hands of some organization? And when an organization is "religious," we can face greater disappointment. How can a Christian organization claim the gospel yet act in such contradictory ways?

Organizations hold enormous power to shape and determine the character and quality of life. But power has many faces; it can serve the common good or it can take the form of hubris, greed, and possessiveness. Organizations can forget, or even reject, their fundamental purposes, so that the work they are engaged in becomes distorted, oppressive, and destructive. And therein lies much of our disappointment and anger: the failure of an organization to live up to its purposes and to serve the mission it claims. Organizations can turn their work into dead repetition whose meaning and value is simply (and often wrongly) assumed. They die, but they do so slowly. Edifices of apparent solidarity and even grandeur can remain standing while the supporting structures deteriorate. Regarding the troubles faced by Benedictine monasteries, medieval historian R. W. Southern notes, "It often happens with ancient institutions that the incrustations of time, however much they may be deplored, come to be valued as the most distinctive feature of the institution."[1] Without discerning what is proper and good in an organization as it relates to its mission, we can take for granted that our treasured ways of working and serving are to be protected and maintained at all costs.

What does stewardship mean in this analysis? Stewards care for organizations—the foundations they rest upon as well as the processes they create to carry out the mission—the policies, finances, projects, and people. For example, stewards of First Church of Plymouth are called upon to care for the congregation's resources so it lives out its mission as a downtown congregation in the midst of a pluralistic and democratic society. What it means to be such a community and to carry forth its work with integrity is part of the ongoing conversation about a congregation's role in the Christian tradition, and religion's role in a secular society. Stewards care for organizations by keeping alive the fundamental reason that define why an organization exists and why it embarks on the work it does.

"We need to understand how much of our lives is lived in and through institutions, and how better institutions are essential if we are to lead better lives. In surveying our present institutions we need to discern what is healthy in them and what needs to be altered, particularly where we have begun to destroy the nonrenewable natural and nearly nonrenewable human resources upon which all our institutions depend."
—Robert Bellah, *The Good Society*[2]

Those who lead our institutions are called upon to be what former seminary president Malcolm Warford calls "stewards of hope" and "stewards of vision." Trustees of religious organizations are responsible for guiding an organization's vision so that it gives "shape to the institution's mission and its programs" and "informs operations of the organization."[3] Being stewards of vision (and I would include here all leaders of the organization) means looking at the organization's life "through their religious and theological resources of tradition, memory, and hope." Rather than relying only on business planning models, Warford argues that religious organizations "need to pursue the fundamental question of who is calling them and what they are called to be. It is through attention to these questions that they will be able to deepen their understanding of their history, mission, and distinctive ways of sorting out the various claims that are made on their resources."[4] One means by which trustees can keep the vision alive, he says, is by asking thoughtful questions. I think one of the essential means of raising questions and finding good answers is through a culture of evaluation as learning.

As Warford points out, some Christians are called into special roles of stewardship because of their positions of leadership (e.g., bishops, presidents, trustees). Yet it is not too much to claim, it seems to me, that all Christians share the common calling to be stewards of religious organizations. We share in the stewardship of resources, which includes care for the materials people create and use, the time they spend in working for the effort, and the people served. This is one reason why good planning and meaningful evaluation are important aspects of stewardship. Obviously, resources are not infinite—money does not grow on trees, people are not contracted to work 100 hours a week, and the necessary materials are not always available. A good plan identifies the resources necessary to properly execute a project and realistically reach its goals. Evaluation further deepens our appreciation for how precious are the gifts God has bestowed on the organization, and identifies how resources can be used more wisely. And finally, evaluation reminds us that we are stewards of one of God's greatest gifts and mysteries—students being taught, campers who are recreating, members joining together in celebration and worship, and the sick being healed.

DISCERNMENT: A VIRTUE OF SEEING

Planning and evaluation involve aspects of discernment, because they call upon our ability to see and analyze well. Step 4 describes the kind of discernment that evaluators are called upon to practice—to describe accurately what is happening in a project and what participation means for the people engaged in the project. Discernment in both planning and evaluation involves keen perception, a kind of seeing that allows us to make distinctions, to see what is obvious and obscure, and to judge what we see. Of course, evaluation is a natural human act, and we do it all the time; the point is that stewards of organizations take the time to do it well. If we do not discern what is happening in our projects and organizations, and why, we risk the chance that our practices become corrupt and harmful to the organization and the people it serves.

"It is a fact of life that what we see depends not only on what is in front of our eyes, but also on what lies within our hearts and minds. . . . Who we are determines what we see. What people see is an indication of what they care about and can care about. It is an indication of the depth and breadth of their compassion, the scope and quality of their loves and desires, and the intensity with which they feel. Our emotions, evaluations, descriptions, predispositions, and desires are all brought to bear in our seeing. Attention is the concentration of the whole self in a moment of time. The quality of that attention is largely determined by the quality of the self who attends."

—Craig Dykstra, *Vision and Character* [5]

Christians describe the word *discernment* as a faithful inquiry into understanding what God is doing and what we are to do in response to God. What is distinctive about Christian discernment is the way Christians come to understand what happens in life through the life, death, and resurrection of Jesus. For example, Christians see every person as made in the image of God. We also see a world filled with failure, misery, and suffering. But Christians understand and accept the fact that people do and will fail—they can stumble, make poor choices, break promises, and do egregious harm to one another, sometimes in the name of good. But these human failings—the sins of individuals and communities—are seen from the vantage point of God's willingness to forgive and reconcile. Christians also see beauty, joy, and success; sins are forgiven, pain is healed, promises renewed, and banquets celebrated. One of the great mysteries Christians proclaim is God's steadfast love that does not abandon the individual or the community. Through participating in Word and Sacrament, Christians are formed by the Jesus story and come to see the world through his eyes. Christian discernment is a communal, not a solo, practice. It occurs in communal prayer and counsel, among Christians who seek together to discern what God is doing and what we are to do in response.

Theologian James Gustafson describes institutions as one of the three communities in which Christians participate (the other two being interpersonal relationships and the culture). Each of these communities constitutes a realm of Christian service, but they also are places where God's creating, sustaining, and ordering activity takes place. In other words, God is active within all realms of human life—even organizations! Gustafson claims that Christians are obligated to discern and interpret God's activity in organizations in order to respond in ways that are faithful, right, and good.

"For what is this institution responsible? How do its purposes cohere with an informed understanding of the manner and ends of life that Christians believe to be consonant with what God is seeking to say and to do? How can persons in institutions act to give direction to their activities so that the well-being of humanity is sustained and improved by the policies and activities of institutions? In the divine economy, institutions and their relations to each other are patterns of social life in and through which moral responsibility—to God, for the human community—are exercised."
—James M. Gustafson, "A Theology of Christian Community"[6]

Gustafson's description of the role of discernment in institutions is similar to my approach to planning and evaluation. Discernment is never general; it always looks toward the particular, concrete material realities of a project. According to Gustafson, institutions "are locations in which man's obligations to God and to other men have a concreteness, a virtually material quality, which expresses man's moral discernment and care."[7] To discern God's activity and our proper response in institutions involves, in Gustafson's terms, "perceptivity, discrimination, subtlety, sensitivity, clarity, rationality, and accuracy."[8] Evaluation means taking a close-up look at organizations and projects. From afar, we may think that a congregation or high school or university looks quite ideal. But on closer inspection, we see that it is a mixture of strengths and weaknesses—and the closer we get the more obvious these become. Discerning planners and evaluators practice a way of seeing into the messy realities of organizations and projects, for this is where God's purposes for creation and God's promises for the world are made real and known.

"Moral discourse, through which the specification of intentions and ends, of words and deeds, can come, enables the church to move with some confidence from the ground affirmations of its faith to be an initiating, directing, active community, with a keen awareness of the marks it ought to hit and of the actions it will take to fulfill its purposes."
—James M. Gustafson, "Two Requisites for the American Church"[9]

PRUDENCE: A VIRTUE OF TAKING ACTION

If discernment is a way of seeing, its close partner is prudence, a way of taking action. St. Augustine describes prudence as "knowledge of what to seek and what to avoid. . . . It is love discerning aright that which helps from that which hinders us in tending to God."[10] If discernment is a guide for action, then prudence is choosing a course of action. Prudence is especially important as leaders discern which projects to pursue and the size and shape of those projects. Religious organizations cannot be all things to all people: choices must be made, usually from among several paths of service that are deemed good and worthy. Prudence helps guide our choices in discerning the right projects and the right size of those projects.

"Be doers of the word, and not merely hearers." —James 1:22

Generally in the moral tradition, prudence involves knowledge about two aspects of a situation—the Christian tradition's basic principles and ideals for moral action, and the particular conditions of a situation. The prudent person does not merely apply universal principles without regard for the situation's particularities; but neither does she look only at the particulars without regard for the more general norms that guide behavior. Knowledge of both is part of prudent action. Prudence strives to find the fitting course of action, which is neither perfect nor absolute in all cases.

"Prudence is properly about the means to an end and its proper work is to set them in due order to the end."
—Thomas Aquinas, *Summa Theologica* II-II [11]

When I look back in the tradition for wise counsel about moral virtues, I usually turn to St. Thomas Aquinas. His description of moral virtues is not only accurate but thorough. In the case of prudence, he identifies eight distinctive parts: memory, understanding, docility, shrewdness, reason, foresight, circumspection, and caution. As was typical of Aquinas's theology, he studied the ancient sources to draw together a comprehensive description of each virtue. These might not be the eight parts of prudence you or I would list, but Aquinas's list draws upon a good deal of wisdom that has merit for planners and evaluators today.

Prudent planners examine conditions by remembering the past and understanding the present. As noted in chapter 1, conditions are multivalent: they have a history and a context that can span many organizations and responses. Understanding the particularities of a condition and a project's response to it requires an accurate and realistic description of what has occurred in the past and what is occurring in the present. Memory and understanding go together especially in religious organizations, where the memory of an entire tradition, as well as the organization's past, come to bear on decisions.

"Lean not on thy own prudence." —Proverbs 3:5

Aquinas chooses docility as part of prudence, which is not a common virtue to most of us but is quite appropriate for planners, evaluators, and leaders. Docility, according to Aquinas, means the prudent person is humble enough "to be ready to be taught." The prudent person is one who takes good counsel in seeking right reason applied to action; and good counsel involves "research proceeding from certain things to others" which is "the work of reason." Evaluation is certainly one of the ways project leaders can seek wise counsel. In a certain sense, evaluators serve as project counselors; they have a special vantage point on a project and can provide means by which others can see and appreciate what is happening and why.

"If you love to listen you will gain knowledge, and if you pay attention you will become wise. Stand in the company of the elders. Who is wise? Attach yourself to such a one. Be ready to listen to every godly discourse, and let no wise proverbs escape you. If you see an intelligent person, rise early to visit him; let your foot wear out his doorstep. Reflect on the statutes of the Lord, and meditate at all times on his commandments. It is he who will give insight to your mind, and your desire for wisdom will be granted." —Sirach 6:33-37

Another aspect of prudence that might not readily come to mind is shrewdness. In Aquinas's terms it refers to taking one's own counsel or "acquiring a right estimate by oneself." We might just say, "Listen to yourself." Project leaders are in a position to be shrewd. Along with project staff, they are the people who are closest to the realities of a project, and they can trust what they know and see.

Aquinas also believes that the prudent person practices foresight and circumspection—views toward the future as well as the means to the end. Foresight means that the prudent person looks into the future to see "that to which things are directed"; in our terms, the project's goals. Circumspection requires the prudent person to see that the means to the end—the objectives, activities, and resources—are good. Of course, project leaders demonstrate foresight when they set realistic project goals. Rather than attempting to predict precisely what will happen in the future, planners and evaluators can remain open to the surprises and possibilities that arise over the course of a project. But this requires that they remain circumspect about the resources and activities. Both resources and activities constitute the means to the end, and project leaders can remain alert to ways in which good and evil "commingle" at every level of a project.

Because prudence deals with "contingent matters of action," there is always the possibility that "evil mingles with good," "good is hindered by evil," and evil takes on "the appearance of good." This is why prudent leaders and evaluators exercise caution: they are neither impertinent, rushing to decision or action prematurely, nor paralyzed into inaction. Caution may mean proceeding slowly and with care. But it also means taking risks at times, even when we do not have all the facts. When an organization decides to take a leap of faith into uncharted waters, caution dictates that it be aware of the risks. Good plans and evaluations can help us see more clearly what should be done next, but prudence requires us to step out and act on the best information we can gather at the moment. In other words, we may have very effective plans and evaluations, but our vision of the situation is never entirely complete.

"The steps that intervene by which one ought to descend in orderly fashion are memory of the past, intelligence of the present, shrewdness in considering future outcome, reasoning which compares one things with another, docility in accepting the opinions of others."
—Thomas Aquinas, *Summa Theologiae* II-II [12]

Jesus taught his followers that true disciples are those that hear his words and act on them. To attend to the foundation as well as to the house requires good stewardship of resources, which means discerning a fitting response and a prudent course of action. We all know what happens to the house built on sand.

"The Bible is a handbook on evaluation from the story of Adam and Eve to the last judgment in the Book of Revelation."
—C. Ellis Nelson, *Using Evaluation in Theological Education* [13]

Despite the growth in the number of abbeys from the founding of Citeaux in 1098 C.E. to 1500 C.E., the Cistercians organizational style did not enjoy lasting success. By 1200, signs of failure were looming: simplicity had given way to wealth and organizational bloat, uniformity had been surpassed by localism, and missionary zeal was replaced by a commitment to organizational maintenance. Other religious orders would come along to pick up where the Cistercians left off. Of course, the Cistercians did not cease to exist, and neither did the Benedictines. In fact, I am writing this book within the walls of a Benedictine monastery that is thriving and stable—a hallmark of its organizational design. Perhaps the tenacity of the Christian life lived out within this particular religious organization over the past 1,500 years comes from its tradition of stewardship, discernment, and prudence. They had a good plan at the start and have created means to reform when the organization wanders far from its original vision. Religious organizations of any kind are never static entities: by virtue of historical circumstances, they change, either by force or by choice. Good planning and evaluation are ways religious organizations can stay at least one step ahead of history and implement change according to their reading of the situation.

NOTES

1. R. W. Southern, *Western Society and the Church in the Middle Ages* (New York: Penguin Books, 1970), 237.

2. Robert N. Bellah et al., *The Good Society* (New York: Alfred A. Knopf, 1991), 5.

3. Malcolm L. Warford, "Stewards of Hope: The Work of Trustees," in Thomas P. Holland and David C. Hester, eds., *Building Effective Boards for Religious Organizations* (San Francisco: Jossey-Bass Publishers, 2000), 6.

4. Ibid., 8.

5. Craig Dykstra, *Vision and Character: A Christian Educator's Alternative to Kohlberg* (New York: Paulist Press, 1981), 50–51.

6. James M. Gustafson, "A Theology of Christian Community," in *The Church as Moral Decision-Maker* (Philadelphia: Pilgrim Press, 1970), 74.

7. Ibid.

8. James M. Gustafson, "Moral Discernment in the Christian Life," in *Norm and Context in Christian Ethics*, Gene H. Outka and Paul Ramsey, eds. (New York: Charles Scribner's Sons, 1968), 19.

9. James M. Gustafson, "Two Requisites for the American Church," in *The Church as Moral Decision-Maker* (Philadelphia: Pilgrim Press, 1970), 155.

10. Thomas Aquinas, *Summa Theologica*, trans. Fathers of the English Dominican Province (New York: Benziger Brothers, 1947), II-II, Q. 49, art. 1.

11. Aquinas, II-II, Q. 49, art. 6.

12. Aquinas, II-II, Q. 53, art. 3.

13. C. Ellis Nelson, *Using Evaluation in Theological Education* (Nashville: Discipleship Resources, 1975), 14–15.

Bibliography

Part I: Project Planning: Five Elements of a Project Design

Wayne Booth and his colleagues have an excellent approach to research and writing arguments in the book *The Craft of Research* (University of Chicago Press, 1995). The authors encourage writers to form an argument based on strong claims and evidence. Even if you are not a student or engaged in writing a research paper or study, the first ten chapters are worth the read; if you are doing research and writing a paper, the entire book is a must.

The way I describe activities, resources, results and impact is influenced by the "program outcome model" developed by the United Way. (See *Measuring Program Outcomes: A Practical Approach*, United Way of America, 1996.) The United Way model is for nonprofit organizations who are required to describe and assess program benefits to participants. Their manual is easy to use and very helpful for basic program planning. See also, "Achieving and Measuring Community Outcomes: Challenges, Issues, Some Approaches" (United Way of America, April 1999).

For a theological approach to describing and interpreting situations, see Edward Farley's chapter, "Interpreting Situations: An Inquiry into the Nature of Practical Theology," in Lewis S. Mudge and James N. Poling, eds., *Formation and Reflection: The Promise of Practical Theology* (Fortress Press, 1987), 1–26.

Part II: Evaluation as Collaborative Inquiry: Six Steps to Effective Evaluation

Craig Dykstra coined the phrase "evaluation as collaborative inquiry" in an essay published in Lilly Endowment's Religion Division newsletter, *Initiatives in Religion* 2, no. 4 (Fall 1993).

A further explanation of the Endowment's philosophy to evaluation can be found in the *Evaluation Notebook* (Lilly Endowment, Inc., 1989). D. Susan Wisely introduces evaluation (5) as a form of continuing education "aimed at expanding moral imagination and enhancing public service." Both "the foundation and its partners" learn through evaluation by enlarging "the context which they conceive and pursue the common good."

Michael Quinn Patton's approach to evaluation is very helpful (*Utilization-Focused Evaluation: The New Century Text*, 3rd ed., Sage Publications, 1997). Patton's material is geared toward the outside evaluator; he says little about how projects are to conduct their own evaluation. However, his "utilization-focused evaluation" is based on the idea that evaluation is as good as its utility. He defines program evaluation (23) as "the systematic collection of information about the activities, characteristics, and outcomes of programs to make judgments about the program, improve program effectiveness, and/or inform decisions about future programming. Utilization-focused evaluation (as opposed to program evaluation in general) is evaluation done for and with specific, intended primary users for specific, intended users."

There are several good guides to designing an evaluation. See, for example, Robert O. Brinkerhoff et al., *Program Evaluation: A Practitioner's Guide for Trainers and Educators* (Kluwer-Nijhoff Publishing, 1983); and *Program Evaluation Kit*, 2nd ed. (Sage Publications, 1987), which includes eight volumes. Volume 3, *How to Design a Program Evaluation* by Carol Taylor Fitz-Gibbon and Lynn Lyons Morris, is particularly helpful.

A refreshing perspective on evaluation of educational programs is Elliot W. Eisner, *The Educational Imagination: On the Design and Evaluation of School Programs*, 3rd ed. (Prentice Hall, 1994). Eisner is helpful in discerning four aspects of evaluation—descriptive, interpretative, evaluative, and thematics. He compares good evaluators to critics and connoisseurs in terms of their capacities to recognize and appreciate qualities of the particular.

The most helpful resource for explaining research and evaluation methods for the nonexpert is Scott Thumma's chapter, "Methods for Congregational Study," in *Studying Congregations*, Nancy T. Ammerman et al. (Abingdon Press, 1998). Thumma is writing for pastors and lay leaders and explains how to use the five methods in congregations.

For guidance in how to formulate survey questions, see Seymour Sudman and Norman M. Bradburn, *Asking Questions: A Practical Guide to Question-*

naire Design (Jossey-Bass Publishers, 1982), and Stanley L. Payne, *The Art of Asking Questions* (Princeton University Press, 1951).

CONCLUSION: DISCERNING AND PRUDENT STEWARDS: THEOLOGICAL PERSPECTIVES ON PLANNING AND EVALUATION

The story about the Benedictines and Cistercians can be found in R.W. Southern, *Western Society and the Church in The Middle Ages* (Penguin Books, 1970), 214–72.

Insights about organizations and institutions are drawn from Robert N. Bellah et al. *The Good Society* (Alfred A. Knopf, 1991).

Malcolm L. Warford's idea of trustees as stewards of hope can be found in "Stewards of Hope: The Work of Trustees," in Thomas P. Holland and David C. Hester, eds., *Building Effective Boards for Religious Organizations* (Jossey-Bass Publishers, 2000), 3–23.

Several essays by James M. Gustasfon are noted: "A Theology of Christian Community" and "Two Requisites for the American Church: Moral Discourse and Institutional Power" in *The Church as Moral Decision-Maker* (Pilgrim Press, 1970), 63–80 and 151–63. See also James M. Gustafon, "Moral Discernment in the Christian Life," in *Norm and Context in Christian Ethics*, Gene H. Outka and Paul Ramsey, eds. (Charles Scribner's Sons, 1968), 17–36.

Craig Dykstra describes "visional ethics" in the book, *Vision and Character: A Christian Educator's Alternative to Kohlberg* (Paulist Press, 1981). See especially chapter 2, "Fundamentals: Visional Ethics."

I have quoted St. Thomas Aquinas from the *Summa Theologica*, trans. Fathers of the English Dominican Province (Benziger Brothers, Inc., 1947). Aquinas's treatment of the moral virtues can be found in the second part of the second part (II-II) at questions 47–170; prudence is discussed in II-II, Q. 47–56.

The quote from C. Ellis Nelson is from *Using Evaluation in Theological Education* (Discipleship Resources, 1975).

Another important source on religious organizations is N. J. Demerath III, et al. *Sacred Companies: Organizational Aspects of Religion and Religious Aspects of Organizations* (Oxford University Press, 1998).

Appendix

Worksheets

WORKSHEET A
Project Workplan: Activities, Schedule, and Resources

Objectives/Activities	Schedule	Personnel	Resources		Costs
			Time		
Objective					
–Activity					
–Activity					
–Activity					
Objective					
–Activity					
–Activity					
–Activity					
Objective					
–Activity					
–Activity					
–Activity					

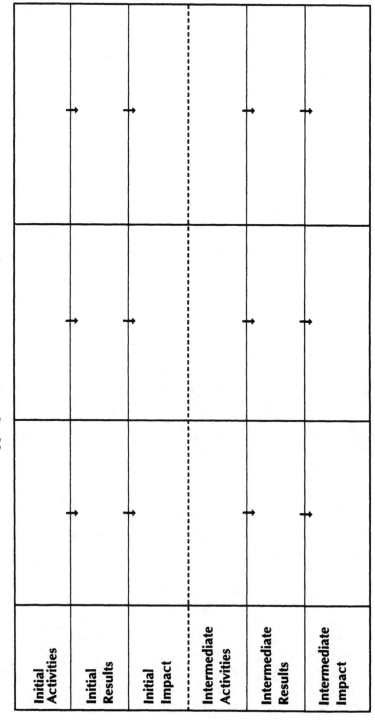

WORKSHEET B
Mapping Activities, Results, and Impact

Initial Activities			
Initial Results			
Initial Impact			
Intermediate Activities			
Intermediate Results			
Intermediate Impact			

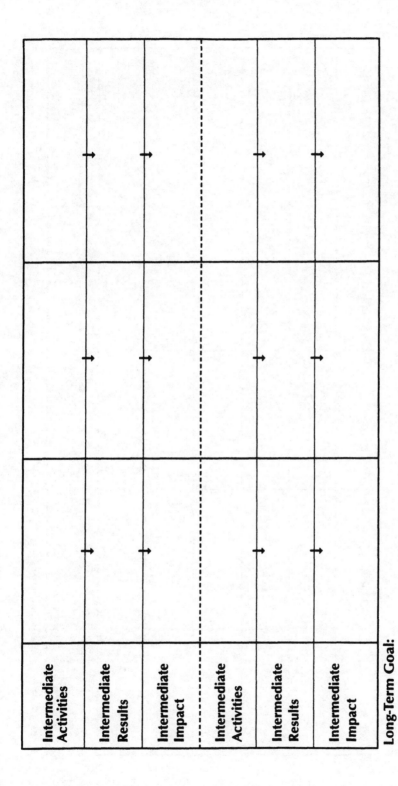

Long-Term Goal:

Worksheet C
Step 1: Focus the Evaluation

Subject	Purpose	Audience	Evaluation Questions	Why is this question important?

WORKSHEET D
Evaluation Design

Purpose/Questions	Data Sources	Methods	Person Responsible	Schedule

Audiences and Evaluation Reports

Audiences	Type of Report	Schedule for Reporting

WORKSHEET F
Evaluation Budget

Budget Category:	Year 1	Year 2	Year 3	Total
Time				
Consultants				
Travel				
Office supplies				
—Telephone				
—Photocopies				
—Mail				
TOTAL				

Made in the USA
Middletown, DE
18 July 2016